ITALIAN
AMERICANS

COMING TO AMERICA

ITALIAN AMERICANS

BARRY MORENO

First edition for the United States, its territories
and dependencies, and Canada published in 2003
by Barron's Educational Series, Inc.

Text © 2003 Barry Moreno
Design © 2003 THE IVY PRESS LIMITED

This book was created by
The Ivy Press Ltd., The Old Candlemakers, Lewes, East Sussex BN7 2NZ, UK

Creative Director Peter Bridgewater

Publisher Sophie Collins

Editorial Director Steve Luck

Design Manager Tony Seddon

Designer Andrew Milne

Senior Project Editor Rebecca Saraceno

Picture Researcher Vanessa Fletcher

All inquiries should be addressed to:
Barron's Educational Series, Inc.
250 Wireless Boulevard
Hauppauge, New York 11788
www.barronseduc.com

International Standard Book No.: 0-7641-5624-1
Library of Congress Catalog No.: 2002108726

Printed and bound in China by Hong Kong Graphics and Printing Ltd
9 8 7 6 5 4 3 2 1

CONTENTS

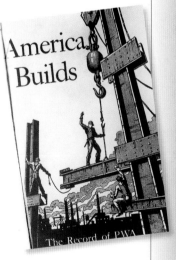

INTRODUCTION

Working at Ellis Island has given me a great deal of insight and understanding into the plight of many immigrant people of the past, and as I reflect on the Irish, the Jews, the Germans, the Poles, and a host of others—I find that none tells the story quite as well as the Italians.

More than four million Italian immigrants came to the United States between 1880 and 1924 and although their migration pattern to the United States seemed "gentle" in comparsion to others, this certainly did not hinder the enormity and vast impact they were to have on American society. Ellis Island holds a special meaning to Italian Americans because through its legendary halls and corridors, the majority of Italians made their first entrance into this country. Of the 12 million immigrants who passed through the station, three million were Italian.

Old pictures and film footage sit in our library's collection and this imagery brings before us a thought-provoking world of the history of immigration. Such images document a past that connects each and every one of us together—either directly or indirectly—with a link in humanity. The eyes of immi-grants show the misery they endured, the sacrifices they made, their uncertain hope, and, lastly, their feeling of confidence for America. The Italian immigration is the classic story of the struggles and obstacles immigrants faced—and still face—as newcomers on America's shores.

For the Italians, part of the difficulty in migrat-ing from home was their love of Italy and their passion for family tradition. Quickly were they to discover that the task of being treated "All men as equal," and the changes needed to blend in to their new society were not as simple as they might have hoped. But for the many who stayed and pros-pered, their quest for a better life was mixed with hardship, satisfaction, and surprise.

The arrival of this culture changed the path of American history, bringing with it a rich heritage, and plenty of ideas to proliferate in this new and unexplored country. The Italian Americans, like other immigrants from many different countries, have without a single doubt made an overwhelming impression on the "New World" with the country itself being named after the early Italian explorer, Amerigo Vespucci.

> ANTHONY MANCINI
>
> On his return home to Italy:
>
> *"I wasn't . . . Italian [anymore]. Neither was I . . . American. I was an Italian-American— a unique breed, an identity in itself."*

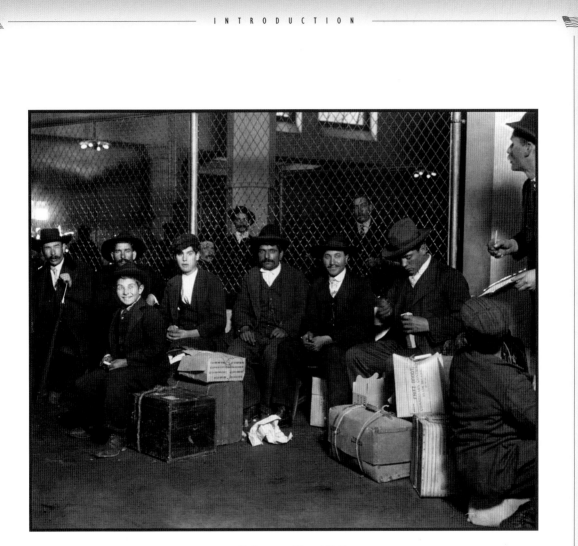

ABOVE: *A group of Italian men and boys, full of hope, awaits*
processing at Ellis Island, sometime around 1905.

OLD ITALY

A Divided People

For centuries Italy had been a divided land. Without a unified central government, most of the country was composed of different kingdoms, principalities, and duchies. By the nineteenth century, the Emperor of Austria controlled much of the North, the King of Sardinia ruled Piedmont (in the northwest), the pope was in charge of a large area in the middle of the country known as the Papal States, and the South—known as the Kingdom of the Two Sicilies—had for many centuries been controlled by a branch of the Spanish royal family.

The Risorgimento

It was in the midst of this widespread disunity that a young Italian named Giuseppe Mazzini (1805–1872) became obsessed with Italian nationalism. He called for the rebirth of Italy as a single united country totally free of foreign domination. Along with Mazzini's *Giovane Italia* (Young Italy) there were two other active groups: the Conservatives and the Moderates. This unification process was given the name *Risorgimento*, which literally means "resurgence." This name was also adopted in 1847 by Count Camillo

LEFT: *Giuseppe Mazzini was a founder of the* Risorgimento, *a revolutionary movement that sought unification and autonomy for Italy.*

BELOW: *A leader of the* Risorgimento, *Giuseppe Garibaldi fought bravely to achieve a united Italy.*

Benzo di Cavour for his newspaper, which became an important voice of the Italian National Movement.

In spite of initial setbacks, including his disastrous invasion of Savoy in 1834 and other fruitless attempts in 1848 and in the 1850s, Mazzini managed to spread his ideas of unification and attract a loyal band of followers. Among them was Giuseppe Garibaldi (1807–1882), a sailor from Nice, who joined Mazzini's Young Italy movement in 1834. After supporting Mazzini's disastrous scheme to seize Genoa, Garibaldi was condemned to death but eluded the police, eventually managing to escape to Brazil. He returned to Italy just in time for the political struggle and insurrections of 1848. At this time King Carlo Alberto, convinced by Cavour that the time was right, declared war on Austria, an act that created a stir of Italian patriotism. The revolutionaries became enthusiastic, and Garibaldi and his companions, for the first time, proudly donned the king's uniform. But this war was not destined to bring glory to Italy: Disaster came instead, with the Italians falling to Austrian forces in the decisive battles of Custozza (1848) and Novarra

ABOVE: *Palermo was one of many Italian cities to see pitched battles in the war against Austria in 1848.*

(1849). The triumphant Austrians were delighted to see King Carlo Alberto abdicate the throne to his son, Vittorio Emmanuelle II, and his exile in Portugal. Meanwhile, in the South Mazzini's army had taken control of Rome, where he proclaimed the creation of an independent Roman Republic, with Garibaldi arriving in support soon afterward. Pope Pius IX, however, called in French troops, who liberated the city after a 30 day siege, after which the regime collapsed. Once again Mazzini and Garibaldi went into exile—Mazzini to London and Garibaldi to New York.

THE KINGDOM OF ITALY: THE TRIUMPH OF THE NORTHERN ITALIANS

The first real inkling of unification came in 1858. Cavour (who was now prime minister in Sardinia-Piedmonte) met with Emperor Napoleon III (the nephew of the great Napoleon Bonaparte and a long-time supporter of Italian unification) to talk about combining the French and Sardinian forces and to defeat the Austrians at Magenta in 1859. This victory, albeit costly, was swiftly followed by Garibaldi's daring and adventurous conquest of the Two Sicilies in 1860. When the Austrians relinquished their hold on Venetia in 1866 and the Papal States lost French military support in 1870, Italy was at last unified. Thus the *Risorgimento* had succeeded brilliantly: The long-sought-for unification of the peninsula into a single nation had been achieved; centuries of disunion and foreign rule were over.

The military hero of the movement, Giuseppe Garibaldi, had loyally handed over the conquests of Sicily and the southern provinces to Vittorio Emmanuelle II, who was now king of a glorious, free, united Italy. However, the real truth was rather different. Italians were profoundly ambivalent about the creation of a unified country. Economic distress in southern Italy became ever more acute, while the Italian government devoted the larger part of the nation's energy and resources to developing northern Italy. Thus the "happy event" of Italian unity seemed to have the reverse effect on the South and drove millions of Italians away from their ancient homeland.

BELOW: *Garibaldi always remained loyal to Vittorio Emmanuelle II, the first king of the unified country.*

LEFT: *Garibaldi's army sailed from Genoa on its way to victory against the Kingdom of the Two Sicilies.*

RIGHT: *Crowds often gathered to listen to political addresses during the tumultuous years preceding Italian unification.*

AMERICA: THE NEW ITALIAN HOPE

THE FIRST ITALIANS IN AMERICA

Despite the fame of Italians such as Christopher Columbus, Amerigo Vespucci, and Giovanni da Verrazano—discoverers and explorers of parts of the New World in the fifteenth and sixteenth centuries—it was a long time before the people of Italy saw America as a land to which they might emigrate. In fact Italian emigration to the region did not really develop until the nineteenth century.

The first Italians who started coming to the English, Dutch, and French colonies of North America in the seventeenth century were mostly from the North of Italy. In the New World they

LEFT: *This map of the world dates from 1570. By then, many Italian explorers had ventured across the oceans to the New World, and the mapmaker used the knowledge of their discoveries.*

RIGHT: *In this fantastical engraving, an Italian explorer, elegantly dressed and carrying a navigational tool, confronts the natives of the New World for the first time.*

made homes for themselves in New Amsterdam, Jamestown, Rhode Island, Connecticut, Pennsylvania, Maryland, and Georgia. One such Italian was Filippo Mazzei (1730–1816), a political philosopher and horticulturist, and a Florentine by birth. He came to America in 1773 at the invitation of Thomas Jefferson, who was fascinated with the idea of producing luxury items such as wine and silk on his plantation in Virginia. Mazzei was an expert on wine grapes and mulberry trees, but in Virginia he became more of a political confidant of Jefferson than the keeper of a vineyard. He was a firm advocate of the liberal ideas of the Enlightenment and the two men soon became friends. When the colonists were debating how far they should go in their quarrel with England,

Mazzei urged them to make a complete break with England and declare their independence. He wrote about his impressions of the conflict between the colonies and the mother country, which Jefferson translated from Italian into English. In one passage, Mazzei states:

" . . . All men are by nature equally free and independent. This quality is essential to the establishment of a liberal government; a truly republican form of government cannot exist except where all men, from the rich to the very poor, are perfectly equal in their natural rights."

Soon the War of Independence broke out, and Mazzei's political involvement increased. The voters of Albemarle County chose him to represent their views at the Virginia legislature in Williamsburg, and in 1780 the Continental Congress sent him to Paris to aid Benjamin Franklin in negotiating a loan from France. His energy and intelligence were helpful not only in attempting to obtain the loan but also in disseminating pro-American views in articles he published throughout Europe. In 1785, two years after establishment of the United States as a free nation, in writing his farewell to Jefferson as he prepared to leave permanently for Europe, Mazzei declared his spiritual love for America as "the asylum of liberty."

BELOW: *From the 1840s, steamships began carrying immigrants across the Atlantic, dramatically shortening journey times.*

THE FIRST MIGRATION: THE NORTHERN ITALIANS 1820–1880

Although small numbers of northern Italians were recorded entering the United States in the first federal immigration records of the 1820s, it was not until the discovery of gold in California in 1848 that Italian immigration began in earnest. This was particularly evident during the 1850s, when 9,231 Italians entered the country, an increase over the previous decade of more than 500 percent! They included artisans, merchants, shopkeepers, winemakers, and farmers, teachers, actors, musicians, dancers, and stonecutters. Many hailed from the rich farming areas of Piedmont, Liguria, and Emilia. Costantino Brumidi was a notable participant in this exodus. He arrived in 1852 and was later deemed as the "Michelangelo" of the United States because of the magnificent fresco paintings he created for the Capitol dome in Washington D.C.

Like all immigrants in those days, the Italians faced considerable hardship to get to their destination. The long sea voyage aboard a sailing vessel was exceptionally miserable. It usually lasted many weeks, and immigrant passengers could generally afford only steerage accommodation. The foulness of the conditions in steerage was notorious and, to make matters worse, the possibility of contracting a contagious disease was high. Common debilitating diseases associated with steerage at that time were cholera, typhoid, and tuberculosis.

CASTLE GARDEN, 1855–1890

The large number of immigrants entering the country through the major port of New York caused a variety of social problems in the city itself because, as mentioned above, many immigrants landed in New York in poor health or with little or no money. For many years port cities like New York, Philadelphia, and Boston had relied on traditional almshouses to care for the destitute and on hospitals to care for the sick. However, many did not survive in such institutions; hospitals could be particularly dangerous because of insufficient medical knowledge about bacteria and contagion, and there was nothing to stop immigrants from seeking shelter in the wretched city slums. The government needed a solution to these social problems, or at least a method to address them. So Castle Garden was established to help organize the arrival process. In the 1840s, 1.5 million immigrants entered the country, the highest recorded number up to that time, with the Irish, German, British, and French topping the lists. Between 1850 and 1890 a total of more than 13 million immigrants entered the United States—an astonishing 8 million of whom came through the country's first immigration depot, Castle Garden.

Located at the tip of lower Manhattan, overlooking New York bay, the Castle Garden Emigrant Depot opened for business on August 3, 1855. Administered by the state of New York, Castle Garden was a circular building that had originally been used as a fortress (1811–1823); it also had had a dazzling career as an auditorium for special events, and then later as a public theater (1839–1855), before being transformed into America's first immigration station.

There were several important advantages in bringing all immigrants to Castle Garden instead of releasing them at the many docks and piers scattered around the city. At this central location they could receive help, travel information, and train or steamboat tickets. Also, they could exchange Old

ABOVE: *Castle Garden, on the tip of lower Manhattan, was the first immigration depot in the United States.*

ABOVE: *From Castle Garden, immigrants dispersed throughout the country. These new arrivals are preparing to head out west. Many Italian immigrants settled in midwestern cities like Chicago (see page 60), and western cities, especially San Francisco (see pages 62–65).*

LEFT: *A hive of activity, Castle Garden accepted more than eight million immigrants between 1855 and 1890.*

World coins such as florins, napoleons, shillings, or marks; send or receive letters; and read postings (some of them written in Italian) on the notice board announcing job vacancies and the locations and prices of local boarding houses. Furthermore, they were fairly safe from thieves and confidence men, and government clerks could record personal information in a more orderly manner.

Castle Garden was a fascinating place, with its staff of 100 employees under a single superintendent. Inside the building, doctors quickly weeded out sick immigrants from the lines of new arrivals and put them aboard a steamboat to be taken to the Verplanck State Emigrant Hospital on Ward's Island in the East River. Everyone else was marched into the central hall, which was known as the Rotunda because of its enormous ceiling. Here the Registering Department clerks, divided into English-speaking and foreign-language-speaking, questioned them, as required under New York State law and recorded their names, nationalities, occupations, and destinations. Up until the 1880s, the services and the help provided at Castle Garden made this port the preferred passage of entry for most Europeans thinking of migrating to the United States. During its heyday, the top five immigrant nationalities processed there were German, Irish, British, Scandinavian (Swedish and Norwegian), and Italian.

Despite its usefulness, Castle Garden's reputation in America declined as the years passed. Various scandals in the 1880s finally forced Congress to intervene in 1890, when it formally notified New York State officials that the federal government had decided to withdraw its recognition and funding of Castle Garden as an immigration depot. It further declared that the federal government would assume all responsibility for the control of immigration. Thus Castle Garden closed its doors on April 18, 1890, ending one of the greatest periods of mass migration to the United States.

ITALIANS AND THE HOMESTEAD ACT

Statistics have shown that the Homestead Act, passed by Congress at the behest of President Abraham Lincoln in 1862, was a further inducement for the Italian people to emigrate. Under its guidelines, the federal government gave 160 acres of land in the midwestern prairies to farmers who promised to build homes there and farm. If they complied, then, after five years, the land would be theirs to keep. Although implementation of this act was delayed by the Civil War, its impact on the national economy over the years 1865–1900 was profound indeed, for the promise of free farmland was hard for many to resist. Hundreds of thousands of Americans from the eastern and southern states were joined by nearly as many European immigrants fresh off the boats in the race to Kansas, Nebraska, Wisconsin, and other prairie states. As well as the long-term economic benefits, there was also a disastrous side. Working the tough prairie soil—soil that had never previously been farmed—was difficult, and the loneliness of prairie life plus the expenses incurred (such as in buying and main-

LEFT: *Many Italians, like these settlers in Nebraska, were drawn to the United States by the promise of free farmland under the Homestead Act.*

RIGHT: *Homesteaders line up to register for farmland in Oklahoma in 1893. More than 36,000 people were allocated land in this makeshift bureau housed in canvas tents.*

taining farm equipment, animals, and a well) made life miserable for some. Under these conditions, a large number of immigrants simply could not last the five years required, gave up on their homesteads, and drifted off to bustling cities and towns like Chicago, Omaha, Milwaukee, and Wichita where better opportunities awaited many of them. And so this diversity of money-making strategies (in the country or in the city) made America ever more attractive to Italians, as the 67,000 immigrants who arrived between 1861 and 1880 could attest.

THE FINEST FARMING LANDS

EQUAL TO ANY IN THE WORLD!!!
MAY BE PROCURED
At FROM $8 to $12 PER ACRE.
Near Markets, Schools, Railroads, Churches, and all the blessings of Civilization.
1,200,000 Acres, in Farms of 40, 80, 120, 160 Acres and upwards, in ILLINOIS, the Garden State of America.

ABOVE: *An old advertisement promises the finest farming land, and an abundance of food. The Homestead Act went one step further with the enticement of free land for all.*

MASS IMMIGRATION
FROM THE MEZZOGIORNO

ABOVE: *Recent arrivals gather their belongings, the city beckons with a new bustling environment—the high-rise New York buildings are visible in the far background.*

THE UNEXPECTED IMMIGRANT

The character of Italian emigration changed drastically after 1880 when landless peasants of the *mezzogiorno* (translated literally as "midday" and used to describe the South of Italy) were made desperate by the grinding poverty and began to leave their country in droves to find work abroad. To the American people, this was unexpected because Italians had never previously formed a large contingent of immigrants to the United States, and as a result the newcomers experienced grudging acceptance as "late arrivals." By contrast, Europeans such as the Germans, the French, and the Scandinavians had been flocking to the United States for decades and shared much the same culture as Protestant America, even to the point of being considered the same ethnic stock and claiming a certain kinship.

The Italians, particularly those from the South, were viewed differently. Their rich Latin culture and Catholic traditions set them apart in American eyes. And because so few Italians had emigrated to the United States in earlier years, it was generally thought that they were not a nation of emigrants. Italian peasants were regarded as conservative people, fiercely devoted to their villages and provinces, as well as to their ancient customs and dialects—people who scarcely ever traveled beyond their native regions and, in spite of their troubles, were genuinely content to live out their lives in the same manner as their forefathers. In addition, Italians were thought to live in a land blessed with a beautiful climate, abundant sunshine, and plenty of pure water and rich soil for farming. This summed up the romantic notion of *la bella Italia*, and reinforced the idea that Italians would never emigrate en masse to any other part of the world. But this ill-informed conception of Italy and the Italians, so common in the 1850s, 1860s, and 1870s, was soon to collapse in the face of a powerful social and economic reality.

RIGHT: *Sicilian peasants who made the journey to America often confronted misunderstanding and prejudice upon arriving in the New World.*

CONDITIONS IN THE MEZZOGIORNO

When Italy eventually became a single nation, the majority of the population hardly considered themselves to be "Italian." Instead, they regarded themselves in a narrower sense, describing each other as purely citizens of their own village, town, or commune (and, sometimes, province). The notion of being "an Italian" scarcely existed for them, and despite the negative aspects of the ancient regime of the Kingdom of the Two Sicilies, the way of life in the *mezzogiorno* had been relatively secure for the peasantry because of aristocratic paternalism, which provided a safety net for the least fortunate in society. In addition, the king kept the national debt and taxes low, food was cheap, and domestic markets were protected from foreign competitors. Thus the southern Italians, nine-tenths of whom were peasants, lived in a poor but stable society, generation after generation, as the years slipped by.

Following unification in 1870, the new Italian government introduced heavy taxation and opened Italian markets to competitive foreign products like wine, thus destabilizing the life of the Italian peasantry. Emigration was the easiest way for millions of Italians to cope with these and other changes that gripped their society and, indeed, the West. Italy's plight was clear. The country had a burgeoning population, the majority of whom had been born in dire poverty, and yet it had few resources. Preeminently an agricultural region, nearly the entire *mezzogiorno* was owned by absentee landlords who still held onto the peasantry and the land, although the remnants of feudalism were fast waning. The peasants had to cope with outdated farming tools, dry land, and natural disasters. They lived under primitive conditions, often having to call "home" a mere hut with no amenities whatsoever. An official description from a U.S. Immigration Commission report in 1911 reads:

ABOVE: *Like these two Neapolitan youths around 1900, Italian peasants lived in extreme poverty after unification.*

"The peasants' huts are mostly low, one-roomed hovels, often with no opening except the door. The floor is of earth or sometimes of stone. The furniture is usually one or two beds, and a bench or wooden chest or chair, and fires are built on a stone hearth. Such animals as the family possesses—pigs, chickens, and perhaps a donkey—share the family quarters, but there is a . . . tendency to have separate dugouts or lean-tos for the donkey and the pigs. . . . Often 8 or 10 people of various ages and both sexes sleep in one or two beds, in the midst of pigs and chickens. Under the beds are stored the produce, usually potatoes and corn, which must support the family through winter. . . ."

Diseases such as malaria and trachoma flourished, and the peasants' diet typically consisted of bread, beans, and onions, as well as vegetables and fruit when in season. Such conditions conspired to create a persistent state of life known as *la miseria*—wretched poverty. Thus it is no surprise that so many Italians embraced emigration with enthusiasm. It fell into their plan of bettering themselves and their families and escaping the hopelessness that seemed to surround them. Their emigration to the United States and other foreign lands, such as Argentina and Brazil, did much to relieve the population explosion in their provinces and gave hope to their families.

23

TIDINGS OF AMERICA:
A HANDFUL OF GOLD

Like other would-be emigrants of the period, the Italians had heard wonderful tales about the United States: that it was a land of infinite possibilities and incomparable wealth, a land where gold could literally be found in the streets, and where the countryside flowed with milk and honey. Rocco Corresco, a young man from Naples, recalled his first tidings of the New World:

ROCCO CORRESCO

First tidings of the New World

"Now and then I had heard things about America—that it was a far-off land where everybody was rich and that Italians went there and made plenty of money, so that they could return to Italy and live in pleasure ever after. One day I met a young man who pulled out a handful of gold and told me he had made that in America in a few days."

The king's passport

In those early days, it was no easy matter for an Italian to leave his country. Aside from enduring the expected emotional stress and the physical and financial strain, one also had to obtain permission from the government.

To obtain this permission, the applicant had to submit a written request for his birth certificate to the town clerk where he was born; this official then forwarded a copy of the document to police headquarters in the provincial capital, where criminal and military service records were kept on file. The police then checked for any crim-inal convictions, records of illegal activities, and military service status—they were especially concerned that an Italian who was due to report for military service might leave the country before fulfilling this obligation. If nothing was found to deny permission to emigrate, a passport could then be issued. This particularly ornate and comprehensive document was inscribed with the king's name and administered at a cost of 2 lire (the government raised the fee to 8 lire in 1901). The money was used to pay for medical examinations at Italian seaports and to provide assistance to Italians abroad.

THE ROAD TO AMERICA

The road to America began at home. Provided with passports, emigrants were then ready to set out for the port of embarkation. The leading ports were Genoa in the North, Naples in the South, and, after 1900, Palermo in Sicily. The main Italian steamship line (before passenger numbers exceeded capacity) was the Navigazione Generale Italiana, whose ships included the *Re Vittorio Emmanuelle*, the *Regina Elena*, and the *Duca degli Abruzzi*. Quoted in Jerre Mangione and Ben Morreale's *La Storia*, one immigrant remembers the trip his family took in 1900, when Sicilians first had to sail to Naples to embark for America:

"We left in a two-wheeled cart that carried a homemade trunk, my mother, two of my brothers. . . . After we got to Palermo . . . we hopped onto a small launch—there was no such thing as a dock. The Mediterranean was very rough. . . . It took all night."

LEFT: *A crowd of emigrants gathers at the steamship landing in Genoa, waiting to board the ship that was to carry them to their new lives in America.*

GENOA

I T A L Y

CORSICA

ROME °°

SARDINIA

NAPLES

m e d i t e r r a n e a n   s e a

PALERMO

SICILY

"VITE ALLO SBARAGLIO"

E. La Riccia
Il messaggero di Sant' Antonio
Dec. 1908, pp. 38-39

"I could not comprehend anything that was happening. . . . Suddenly a young man . . . with a yellow ticket in his cap, his arms outstretched, ran up asking me for help. A sack of his had been taken and his wife and children were missing. Without hesitation, I plunged into that Babylonian confusion of people, goods, and carts. The air was thick with yells, cries, and profanities from almost every dialect in Italy. After considerable searching and effort we succeeded, God only knows how, in locating his family and the delinquent, who was strolling about with the sack on his shoulder. A lively fist-fight broke out during which I received and delivered a number of well-placed blows. A gentleman came to our aid not a moment too soon, grabbed that rascal by the throat, and dragged him over to the police. Once it was over we began to shake and cry uncontrollably. They because of their desperate condition and I because of my rage."

Naples and Genoa were cities with bustling activity at the docks. Crowds of emigrants, officials, and vendors of all sorts of items—from refreshments to grass ropes—could be seen. Genoa, in particular, had a notorious reputation as emigrants were the prey of criminals, confidence men, and other shady characters (see adjacent quotation, the title roughly translates as "Lives at Risk").

ABOVE: *Between the years 1892 and 1924, millions of Italians would exit their homeland, for the long, arduous, and uncertain journey to America.*

THE SEA VOYAGE

The number of emigrants leaving southern Italy was soon so high that the Navigazione Generale Italiana simply did not have enough ships to meet the demand. The major northern European steamship companies, understanding the possibilities of great profit for themselves in servicing this emigration, quickly filled the void and reassigned their older vessels to work the Mediterranean ports. The leading German, French, and also British steamship companies all assigned steamers to the Naples–New York route. Though most Italians came to the United States directly from Italy, many others departed from French, English, or Argentine ports. In the 1890s the cost of the trip varied from $10 to $35, depending on the price wars between the steamship lines; but, after the turn of the century, the price stabilized to about $25 to $30. The sailing season was chiefly from March to October. Steerage and third-class accommodations were the preferred way to travel because much money was saved—something that was vital to the frugal emigrants. Opinions about steerage aboard the different ships varied considerably: Some found it agreeable, whereas others did not. Whether it was good or bad, most emigrants realized that it was the only way to get to America. In April 1891 Francesco Ventresca, emigrating from the Abruzzi, traveled as a steerage passenger aboard the majestic French liner *La Champagne*:

RIGHT: *Italian children aboard their ship, their attention is captured by something in the distance.*

"There were over a thousand of us on board. I recall only steerage. . . . Most of us were assigned to bunks. . . . We managed to get a bit of light through the hatchway or portholes. No one could stay below for very long. We were on the deck, except at night and in stormy weather—we had plenty of that. We ate our three meals a day in groups of six. One man was given a pan and got the food whilst we looked for a good spot on deck. We just crouched like the Orientals. We could not very well say that we enjoyed the food, for only genuine hunger could have made it palatable, and in this case hunger was the best sauce."

In 1902, an American journalist named Broughton Brandenburg, posed as an emigrant to truly experience life in steerage aboard an Italian ship. He was assigned to a compartment that held 200 persons, with double-tiered, iron-framed bunk beds and iron slats supporting burlap mattresses stuffed with straw or grass. Additionally, each passenger was issued a short blanket made of jute; many used their cork life preservers as pillows. He describes the quarters as poorly ventilated and hot. There was a heavy odor of oil and disinfectant, the stink of vomit, and a smell from scraps of rotting food. The noise from the heavy engines droned on amid the cry of babies and the food rations were Neapolitan macaroni, chunks of beef, bread, boiled potatoes, and red wine. *Mal di mare* (seasickness) was one of the dreaded parts of the voyage, its intensity made worse by the rocking and tossing of the vessel during storms.

ABOVE: *After World War I, Italian veterans who fought for the U.S. Army were allowed special dispensation to return. Here, they celebrate their arrival in New York.*

RIGHT: *Having been refused entry, these would-be immigrants wave a sad goodbye to friends on the dock at Ellis Island, as they prepare to board the ship that will return them to Italy.*

ELLIS ISLAND (1892–1954)

The arrival in New York harbor, with the first views of the Statue of Liberty and the tall buildings of Manhattan, was an exhilarating moment for the immigrants looking out from the ship. But at the back of their minds was the uneasy realization that on entering America, they would have to convince the immigration inspectors at Ellis Island—known to the Italians as *Isola della Lacrime* ("island of tears")—that they would cause no trouble and were worthy of being there.

After passing quarantine, the steamship from the Mediterranean was met by officials from Ellis Island who were ready to inspect it. Meeting the ship's officers, the officials obtained the required information, including details about sick passengers and tips about suspicious ones. The boarding

RIGHT: *A mother and her three children, exhausted from the long sea journey, search for their luggage at Ellis Island in 1905.*

clerks looked over the ship's passenger list and made a complete handwritten copy of it to be taken straight to Ellis Island.

As the weary yet excited immigrants disembarked at Ellis Island, officials known as "groupers" shouted to them to form two lines: women and children in one, and men in the other. Each person was tagged with a slip of paper, often color-coded to indicate the steamship line, inscribed with a manifest number, the name of the steamship, and the immigrant's name. These strict procedures, often unnerving to immigrants, were crucial to the crowd control techniques that had been developed as a matter of necessity at the world's busiest immigration station. There could be as many as 2,000 people disembarking at any one time, and so it was essential to maintain order.

First step: Medical inspection

Doctors, who worked for the U.S. Public Health Service, then began the medical examination procedure famously known as "line inspection."

One doctor examined the immigrants' eyes for any visual impairment or sign of disease. Other doctors had a special technique to identify signs of poor health called the "six-second physical." Standing at a point where the line of immigrants made a sharp turn, a doctor could observe an immigrant from three angles: front, profile, and rear. This let him scrutinize the immigrant's gait, posture, and mannerisms. Next came an examination of the scalp and neck for signs of diseases such as favus or goiter and for head lice. The doctor also tried to detect signs of mental instability—although the method for this was hardly fail-safe—by startling the immigrant with questions. The immigrant's reaction was supposed to give an inkling of the person's mental state.

Upon completion of a full examination, a medical certificate was issued and cosigned by three doctors. Immigrants found to be very sick or dangerously ill were hospitalized at once and only after receiving medical care were they sent on to undergo the immigration inspection.

Second step: Immigration inspection

The main immigration inspection took place in the Registry Room. Federal law required the immigration inspector to exclude aliens (the term applied

ABOVE: *Medical officers examine recent immigrants at Ellis Island in 1911. The eye examination, seen here, could reveal signs of many different diseases.*

RIGHT: *In the "Great Hall" immigrants received their main immigration inspection. Inspectors asked a number of probing questions and also studied the documentation that immigrants brought with them from Italy.*

FRANCESCO
MARTOCCI

Italian immigrant and later
immigration inspector

*"... Here in the main
building, they were
lined up: a motley
crowd in colorful
costumes, all ill at
ease and wondering
what was to happen
to them."*

LEFT: *This dormitory housed women and children who were detained on Ellis Island following immigration inspection. After further investigation, the vast majority of detainees were eventually admitted to the United States.*

to foreigners) suffering from any dangerous or contagious medical condition. Also excluded were convicted criminals, dangerous radicals and anarchists, polygamists, prostitutes, and those guilty of moral turpitude. Medical certificates, testimonials of good character, and warning telegrams from foreign police forces were all examined. There was also a restriction barring all persons "liable to become a public charge," a sweeping category that included vagabonds, professional beggars, unescorted women and girls, underage boys, and physically feeble persons. With these considerations at hand, the inspector, sitting at a high desk at the front of the line typically asked 29 questions, such as What is your name? Age? Occupation or calling? Race? Country of origin? Do you under-

stand English? Speak it? Read it? Write it? What are the name and address of your next of kin abroad? Have you ever been to the United States before? What is your destination? By whom was your fare paid? Are you a contract laborer?

About 80 percent of the immigrants passed inspection and were free to go down to the ground floor to wait for a ferry to transport them to Manhattan or to the Jersey City railway terminal. Of those who were not immediately accepted, half were sent to the hospital for medical treatment, and the other half were detained for legal reasons. Most detainees had no more than an overnight stay: some had to wait for money to be cabled to them; others were waiting for husbands, fathers, or guardians to pick them up; and others were waiting for information, such as the confirmation of an address. Any immigrant who aroused suspicion faced more scrutiny or a hearing before a Board of Special Inquiry.

Those who were detained waited hours, days, and sometimes weeks before receiving a decision—although the vast majority were eventually admitted. During their detention, men and women stayed in separate quarters; children were kept with their mothers. Immigrants in such a predicament sorely needed help, and organizations such as the Italian Welfare League and the Society for the Protection of Italian Immigrants were formed to meet this need. Missionaries, volunteers, and social workers also provided assistance, and Roman Catholic priests not only offered spiritual guidance—hearing confessions and singing mass—but also helped immigrants to get sponsors or money and wrote or read letters.

THE DECLINE OF ELLIS ISLAND

Italian immigration dropped severely after passage of the restrictive Immigration Acts of 1921 and 1924, which were directed against the mass migration of Italians, Slavs, and Jews. Italy, which had previously sent hundreds of thousands of immigrants each year, received a quota of 42,057 per annum under the 1921 law and only 3,845 per year under the 1924 law.

The Ellis Island immigration station closed in 1954 and was declared a national monument in 1965. In the 1970s, Peter Sammartino convinced the National Park Service to oversee a small cleanup job on the island, which allowed it to be opened for tours (1976–1984). Finally, President Ronald Reagan supervised a full-scale restoration of the island's main building and its reopening as the Ellis Island Immigration Museum in 1990; Reagan persuaded Lee A. Iacocca, chairman of the Chrysler Corporation, to spearhead fundraising for the project. It seems fitting that in the end, two Italian Americans, Sammartino and Iacocca, were leaders in the effort to preserve the remains of the immigration station that was truly the "golden door" for the vast majority of Italian immigrants.

LEFT: *Having passed inspection, this Italian family has boarded the ferry that will take them from Ellis Island to the southern tip of Manhattan.*

GREENHORNS

"BIRDS OF PASSAGE"

In contrast to other immigrants, most Italians did not come to the United States with the intention of staying; they were merely following the old European migrant labor custom, according to which gangs of agricultural laborers left their own countries journeyed in search of seasonal work. This practice had been going on for centuries. However, the transatlantic migration pattern of the Italians was an innovation. Previously workers had gone no farther than a neighboring country such as France, but with advances in navigation technology, Italians were able to travel much farther.

Until 1870, sailing to the New World had been long, arduous, and uncertain and usually required weeks. Furthermore, most vessels did not have proper accommodations for large numbers of passengers, and the voyage in steerage was particularly harrowing. Uncleanliness, sickness, and the poor quality of the food and water were also problems. Gradually, steamships reduced the length of the ocean crossing to a week or ten days, and by the end of the nineteenth century, the newest ships could traverse the Atlantic in just five days. This fitted in with the work cycle of itinerant laborers, and with the relatively high wages offered in America, migrant workers began to flock to the

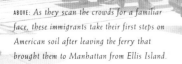

ABOVE: *As they scan the crowds for a familiar face, these immigrants take their first steps on American soil after leaving the ferry that brought them to Manhattan from Ellis Island.*

United States. Most were *contadini*, landless peasants from the *mezzogiorno*, aged between 18 and 45, who found work as common laborers with picks and shovels. They came to work for a short time (the average length of stay was three to five years for most), save money, and return home to invest it somehow or to help their families. Thus the nature of their immigration tended to be transient, and when the jobs disappeared, they left as quietly as they had come, sailing back to Italy or to another country, such as Brazil, Venezuela, or Australia, in search of other jobs.

Because of the high rate of Italian immigration at the time, this cyclic system could not fail to attract the attention of American officials, as well as journalists, critics, and ordinary citizens. It departed drastically from the ideal of immigration: Americans had assumed that most immigrants came to their country seeking freedom, only to find that this was not necessarily true. Americans labeled these kinds of migrants "birds of passage," a term that became almost synonymous with southern Italian immigrants, although other countries behaved similarly during the 1880–1930 period. The rate of departure among Italians was 50 percent, although their return rate was rivaled and even exceeded by that of Hungarians, Turks, Greeks, Bulgarians, and Spaniards.

PADRONE SYSTEM

Itinerant workers were common at Ellis Island; some passed through the immigration station as many as ten times and were able to warn and advise other *paesani* about what to expect there and how to answer the inspector's questions. This advice was worth its weight in silver (if not gold) to greenhorns, and plenty of lire were paid for this service. These advisors/agents became known as *padroni*, and in the 1880s and 1890s they played a key role in bringing the *contadini* to America, for these experienced immigrants acted as guides and protectors for the newcomers.

ABOVE: Padroni, *experienced Italian immigrants, helped new arrivals to find jobs, lodgings, and even lent them money in the first few days.*

TOP: *Conditions often were harsh—this Italian woman shelters in a basement with her baby, waiting for her husband to return with some food.*

BOTTOM: *Even children found employment in New York. These boys are peddling bread on Mulberry Street in New York City's Little Italy around 1900.*

ABOVE: *Boys could also earn money polishing shoes on the streets of Manhattan's affluent neighborhoods.*

As the demand for Italian immigrant workers grew with America's industrial growth, the *padroni* were contracted as agents both by immigrants and by large number of American businesses. The steady stream became a flood of immigrant workers offering cheap labor, who needed someone to find them jobs. Although the *padroni* were useful to both parties, it was the immigrants who became especially dependent on them in this strange land, for the *padroni* calmed their fears, arranged their lodging and transportation, sometimes lent them money, and, of course, found jobs for them. Consequently, the role of the *padrone* was vital in bringing over thousands of Italians because he took responsibility for their welfare. The sense of security that *padroni* provided made emigration popular and encouraged more and more Italians to try their luck in America. However, as with all systems of this kind there was a black side too. Many *padroni* took advantage of the helplessness and ignorance of their fellow countrymen by charging excessively for expenses and preventing them from setting out on their own. Despite this, the system worked. One prominent *padrone* was Ligurian-born Luigi Fugazy (1839–1930). Having gained considerable wealth through aiding his fellow countrymen, he was able to build up profitable businesses as a banker, operator of a steamship agency, and an employment office. Fugazy organized Italian mutual benefit societies and even obtained some political influence among the Irish bosses in Tammany Hall.

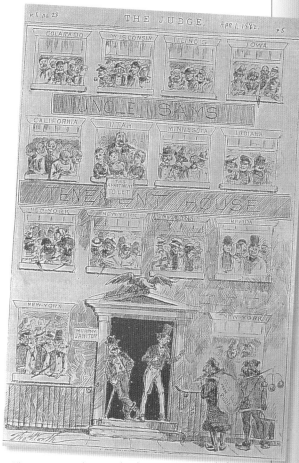

ABOVE: *This cartoon image depicts two homeless immigrants in search of a bed in "Uncle Sam's Tenement House." They were often overcrowded, depressing places for the underprivileged.*

LABOR

To the Italian immigrant, America was a worker's paradise, for most of the time jobs abounded. The typical work of immigrants was pick-and-shovel labor. *Padroni* and bosses organized work gangs and supervised the daily grind. Long before he gained recognition as an author, Constantine Panuzio worked as a common laborer. Many years later he recalled how he and a French sailor named Louis learned about work while staying in a boarding house in Boston's North End:

"... We began making inquiries about jobs and were promptly informed that there was plenty of work at 'pick and shovel.' We were given to understand by our fellow-boarders that 'pick and shovel' was practically the only work available to Italians. Now these were the first two words I had heard and they possessed great charm. ... I practiced for a day or two until I could say 'peek' and 'shuvel' to perfection. Then I asked a fellow-boarder to take me what the work was like. ... He did. He led me ... to where some work was going on, and there I did see with my own eyes what the 'peek and shuvel' were about. My heart sank within me, for I had thought it some form of office work; but I was game and since this was the only work available for Italians, and I must have money to return home, I would take it up."

The majority of men sought work in construction—the building of the Statue of Liberty, as well as its foundations and pedestal (1883–1886), was largely the work of Italian laborers. Additionally, thousands of Italians worked on the construction of subway lines, dug tunnels, paved streets, and toiled in factories; others were tailors, barbers, greengrocers, hawkers, bootblacks, and ragpickers, as well as organ grinders with the inevitable monkey on the shoulder. These were common sights in old New York.

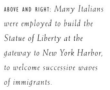

ABOVE AND RIGHT: *Many Italians were employed to build the Statue of Liberty at the gateway to New York Harbor, to welcome successive waves of immigrants.*

RIGHT: *Italians were involved in major construction projects not just in New York City [main picture] but also throughout the country. These laborers [right] are preparing the ground for a new railroad in upstate New York.*

LEFT: *An Italian laborer walks down the tracks carrying his tools. Around ten percent of Italian immigrants found work with the gangs that built America's network of railroads.*

RIGHT: *Many Italian women took in sewing to do at home, where their children were often enlisted to help out.*

Italians with experience in tailoring found plenty of work in New York—one of the leading centers of the clothing industry. Many Italians also obtained lower-level positions as sewing machine operators and pressers. Italian housewives often earned five cents an hour by working at home as garment finishers, while single women found employment in garment workrooms and factories. Little or no safety precautions were taken for the immigrants working in often extremely over-crowded factories. One such death trap was the Triangle Shirtwaist Company, located on the three top floors of a ten-story building in New York's Greenwich Village. In March 1911 a fire broke out and quickly spread, the flames engulfing the huge piles of cloth, fabrics, and laces. The workers—mostly poor Italian and Jewish immigrant women—were caught in the conflagration and

could find no safe way to escape because the stairwell was blocked. Trapped and panic-stricken, many of the workers leaped from the factory windows to their death into the street below, their hair and clothes ablaze. In all, 146 people were killed. The repercussions of this tragedy were great and forced the state legislature and the governor to enact numerous labor laws governing the protection of workers.

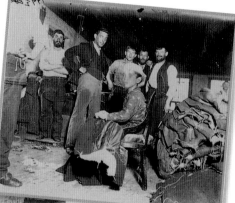

ABOVE: *Many men and boys were also employed in the garment business. Here, they make leather coats in a sweatshop based in their rooming house.*

LEFT: *Factories were a main source of work, but they also often had poor health and safety conditions, some leading to serious infernos.*

Italians also found work in railroad gangs, as strikebreakers in mines and factories, as cigar makers in Florida, and as farm laborers in New Jersey, Louisiana, Arkansas, and California. Women became textile workers at home, in clothing factories, and in mills like those of Lawrence and Lowell in Massachusetts.

SOME LEADING JOBS OF ITALIAN IMMIGRANTS: 1890 CENSUS	
1. Laborers	34%
2. Railroad workers	10%
3. Miners/quarrymen	8%
4. Merchants	6%
5. Farm laborers	4%
6. Peddlers	3%
7. Barbers	3%
8. Boot/shoe makers	3%
9. Tailors	2%
10. Farmers	2%

ABOVE: *Having laid the tracks, Italian laborers run a supply cart along them, the first vehicle to travel those rails, to bring new materials to the end of the line, around 1900.*

CHAIN MIGRATION

Regarding themselves mainly as sojourners, many Italians vigorously resisted joining organizations or associations such as a trade union, a local Catholic parish, or any group asking for membership dues. They were extremely thrifty and carefully saved their earnings, sending as much money back to Italy as they could. These remittances became the lifeblood for family members back home and helped to improve the Italian economy. They also made America more alluring to those who had not yet arrived there. As a result, the "chain migration" that had been evident before began to increase. This term describes the tendency of immigrants to send for sons, brothers, uncles, nephews, cousins, and friends from their own villages and towns, in a continuous flow. This close link between Italians from similar villages increased the stream of people from Molise, Campania, Calabria, Naples, Basilicata, Sicily, Sardinia, and the North of Italy.

About 20 percent of this flow of immigrants usually comprised women, and as time passed, the percentage of female immigrants increased significantly as married men sent for wives and daughters and bachelors sent for girls whom they hoped would become their future brides. The preference for an Italian bride created a remarkable phenomenon: Between 1900 and 1930 large numbers of

LEFT: *Once they established themselves in the New World, many Italian men sent for their wives to join them. Others wrote home in search of young girls whom they could marry. These women wait apprehensively in Ellis Island in 1910, many of them about to meet for the first time the man they are to marry.*

RIGHT: *Italian immigrants did not forget those they left behind. Here, in 1936, the Agnese family welcomes their grandmother, who is meeting her 40 grandchildren for the first time.*

"picture brides" received steamship tickets from would-be husbands who then anxiously awaited their fiancées' arrival. The encounters at Ellis Island could be disappointing, however—sometimes on both sides. More often young women found that their husband-to-be was not the handsome fellow in the photograph but someone entirely different. Maud Mosher, a former Ellis Island matron, described one such encounter in an article that she wrote for the *Coming Nation* in 1910:

COMING NATION 1910

Maud Mosher

"The Italian interpreter came running into the room and called out, 'Matron wanted in the Discharging Division at once, quick!' I went on the run, thinking something had happened and wondering what it could be. There was this Italian girl crying and trembling and an old ugly Italian man saying she was his 'marita.' You know how they say it, 'mea marita, mea marita.'

"The girl was saying just as vehemently, 'No-a marita, no-a marita.' The Inspector said to me, 'take this girl somewhere.' The man started to come around the desk, but the interpreter and a gateman took hold of him. I took the girl into the back room of the Temporary Detention division and sat [her] down and stayed with her awhile until she had quieted down."

RIGHT: *Although conditions for new immigrants were difficult, they did not stop hoping and striving for a better life, as imagined in this scene from a play shown in Little Italy in 1902.*

Thankfully, the story ended happily when the girl was united with her true husband, a young man whom she had only seen in a photograph (they had been married by proxy). The husband had been hurt in an accident, and his personal effects—including the details of his wife's imminent arrival in America—had been stolen by a coworker, the "ugly" man described in the article. Many encounters—though usually less melodramatic—occurred at Ellis Island as couples were reunited after years apart or immigrants met those whom they had never previously seen.

New homes for old

This broadening of chain migration added a new and vital element to the Italian story, for the migration of women caused men to take on more settled habits, with the establishment of house-holds, especially in urban areas like New York, Philadelphia, and Chicago. This encouraged more and more Italians to choose to remain in America. Of course, in some cases dissatisfied women often forced their husbands to go back to Italy with them, but if not, the families found cheap lodgings in tenements near their jobs, preferably within walking distance. They typically lived in buildings where plenty of other *compari* lived, as well as other immigrants—often Irish, Jews, or Poles. Italians were known to be clannish, and Italians from one part of Italy often did not mix well with those from another part of the country. This resulted in tenement buildings or whole street blocks that were exclusively Sicilian, Roman, or Neapolitan, or, even more typically, inhabited by people from a certain town or village such as Caserta or Piacenza.

ABOVE: *Once the family was reunited, many Italian immigrants left the crowded conditions of Manhattan for new neighborhoods that held the promise of better living conditions. This family found a comfortable home in Providence, Rhode Island.*

LITTLE ITALIES

COMING TO TERMS WITH LA MERICA

W hen large numbers of Italians settled in American towns and cities, they preferred to live among their own kind, creating close-knit neighborhoods that were rich in Italian culture. Each of these communities was called a "Little Italy," and they flourished for decades, meeting the needs of immigrants for a home away from home where they would be unassailed by doubt, prejudice, or fears. In these neighborhoods there were *paesani* with the same feelings and appreciations, people who understood the need to recapture the old life in a strange land.

But a Little Italy was all too often an over-crowded community with grim tenements, smelly boarding houses, and a mishmash of small businesses such as bakeries, cheese shops, stores selling second-hand goods, and taverns. Its streets were filled with men selling fresh fruit and vegetables from pushcarts, women going about their errands, and children playing everywhere. In the heat of summer, ice-cold Italian *gelato* was doled out sparingly on brown wrappers to a delighted throng. Every community had a factory that produced a variety of pasta, always loved by the Italians. But pasta—or macaroni, as it was then commonly

RIGHT: *Every "Little Italy" boasted at least one Italian-language newspaper, which published news from Italy as well as from other Italian-American communities across the United States.*

known—did not impress the Irish, Germans, or Americans, who discounted this Italian food as slight in comparison to potatoes, bread, and meat.

Catholic churches and settlement houses were institutions that provided help for the newcomers, as did Italian-language newspapers bearing such names as *L'Eco d'Italia* in New York, *L'Italia* in Chicago, and *L'Eco della Colonia* in Los Angeles. These newspapers offered Italians their own advertising medium, enabling them to promote Italian culture and at the same time acted as sounding boards for their readers' many complaints and frustrations concerning *La Merica*.

LEFT: *Mulberry Street, seen here in 1900, was the heart of New York City's Little Italy.*

ITALIANS OF NEW YORK

The first important Italian settlement in New York was located in the notorious Five Points neighborhood in the 1840s. But as more Italians arrived, the community crept slowly northward and finally found its richest cultural expression in the immigrant world of Little Italy. This area lay between Houston Street to the north and Canal Street to the south, and between Mulberry Street to the east and Broadway to the west. The consecration of the churches of St. Anthony of Padua in 1866 and Our Lady of Pompeii in 1892 testifies to the sizable extent of the Italian population. By this time, Piedmontese and Tuscans could be found on the Lower East Side, and Genoese, Calabrians, Neapolitans, and Sicilians in Greenwich Village. By 1910, more than 500,000 Italians lived in New York, many of whom eventually returned to Italy. Mono Cino, whose family moved to Little Italy in 1910, recollects:

ABOVE: *In New York's Little Italy, a family works together around the dining table making artificial flowers.*

"We lived in a small short alley, it's still there, called Extra Place, near the Bowery on First Street. I remember the cobblestones, and you could smell what everybody was cooking. The halls were lit by gas; and the toilets, made of cast iron, were in the halls."

As mentioned on page 40, the majority of Italians worked as unskilled laborers in areas such as construction and street work; others were employed as tailors, janitors, shoeshine men, and bricklayers. But in New York, in spite of a predominance of menial labor, a growing minority of workers could be found in the professional class: pharmacists, physicians, lawyers, dentists, schoolteachers, and architects. There were also many Italian landlords, small-time agents who remitted funds to Italy, several important immigrant savings banks, and two Italian steamship lines with twice-weekly sailings to the old country. Italian women found work in various industries: dressmaking and manufacturing artificial flowers for hatmakers, as well as making silks and laces, candies, cigars, and paper. When the work was home-based, the women enlisted the help of their daughters and other family members. But living in New York City did not prevent Italians from setting up small gardens on vacant lots and abandoned land, where in the summer they raised vegetables and kept chickens.

Another district that became a mecca for Italians was East Harlem, located in the northeastern part of the city. This area, noted for its affordable housing, quickly emerged as a second Little Italy, and by 1930, about 80,000 Italians were living there. Catholicism, combined with Italian folk traditions, was richly present in religious celebrations. This community also developed a vibrant political culture and later achieved some influence through its own Italian-American congressmen,

Fiorello LaGuardia (1923–1933), James J. Lanzetta (1933–1935, 1937–1939), and Vito Marcantonio (1935–1937, 1939–1951). By 1960, however, many Italians had moved out of East Harlem, and this area became a predominantly Hispanic quarter.

Italians also established a colony in Brooklyn when it was still an independent city, back in the 1850s, but settlements did not really become significant until after 1900. By the 1920s, Italians from Little Italy and other parts of Manhattan began moving to apartment buildings in Bensonhurst; this process continued well into the 1950s, when Italian Americans were joined by newcomers from Sicily, Calabria, and Naples. By 1980, 80 percent of the population of the neighborhood was Italian, with

ABOVE: *Fiorello LaGuardia, the son of an Italian immigrant, was one of New York City's most charismatic mayors, serving three terms.*

ABOVE: *Vito Marcantonio, shown here speaking at a rally in 1949, was one of the first Italian-American congressmen.*

ABOVE: The "face" of New York was one of opportunity and prosperity. The reality for many was very different, but from here, they could travel elsewhere in the country to try their luck.

a large proportion of Sicilian culture as evidenced by the annual feast of Santa Rosalia, the patron saint of Sicily, and by the many Sicilian restaurants. Another Brooklyn community, Greenpoint, is famous for its ten-day Feast of Our Lady of Mount Carmel, during which Italian-American men compete for the honor of carrying the famous tower known as the *giglio* (lily) through the streets. Two other neighborhoods of interest are Coney Island and Flatbush. After 1900 a number of Italians started to settle in Coney Island and eventually they founded the parish church of Our Lady of Solace. Flatbush was the location of the principal cemetery for Italian Catholics, giving rise to the negative expression *andare a flabusse*.

Small numbers of northern Italians, like candlemaker and original inventor of the telephone Antonio Meucci and political exile Secchi de Casale, settled in Rosebank, Staten Island, by the end of the 1840s. It was in Meucci's house that Garibaldi spent his year of exile, and during this time Meucci tried to help other political refugees (often to his own detriment). Then, the 1880s saw the first arrival of southern Italians on the island. Although many were initially interested in farming there, most went into other occupations and settled in Rosebank, which soon took on the Italian character that it still has today. Thanks to the opening of the Verrazano Narrows Bridge in 1964, Staten Island began to attract more and more Italians, and today 50 percent of the residents of the borough are of Italian ancestry, giving it the largest concentration of Italians in New York City.

Famous New York Italians include Jimmy Durante, Charles Atlas, Lucky Luciano, Anne Bancroft, Paul Gallico, Tony Bennett, Rocky Marciano, and Martin Scorsese. Politicians include three mayors of New York—Fiorello LaGuardia (1934–1945), Sicilian-born Vincent Impellitteri (1950–1953), and Rudolph Giuliani (1993–2001)—as well as Senator Alphonse D'Amato, Governor Mario Cuomo, and vice presidential candidate Geraldine Ferrarro.

After World War II, more and more young Italians moved away from the community, and by 1968 Chinatown had absorbed much of what had once been New York's Little Italy; by the 1990s the area was reduced to a bare remnant. However, in spite of its diminished size, Little Italy maintains a vibrant cultural and commercial life. Its annual feast of San Gennaro (patron saint of Naples) in September, as well as its restaurants, bakeries, and stores, attract thousands of Italian Americans, New Yorkers, and tourists from all over the world.

ITALIAN IMMIGRANT POPULA- TION: NEW YORK CITY. ("IMMIGRANT" REFERS TO THOSE BORN IN ITALY.)	
1855	1,039
1860	1,067
1870	3,019
1880	13,411
1890	49,514
1900	145,433
1910	340,765
1920	390,832
1930	440,250
1940	409,489
1950	344,115
1960	281,033
1970	212,160
1980	156,413
1990	90,339

LEFT: *New York's Little Italy was home at one time to numerous celebrated entertainers, including singer Tony Bennett, comic Jimmy Durante, and actress Anne Bancroft.*

ITALIANS OF PHILADELPHIA

After New York, Philadelphia was the nation's leading seaport, and by 1890 it had one of the largest populations of Italian immigrants in the country. In addition to those who first landed in the city, southern Italians were also brought to the Pennsylvania coalfields in 1874 as strikebreakers and were eventually joined by others who were brought in by *padroni* (*see page 37*) as railroad laborers. In the south of Philadelphia, the Little Italy, around Christian Street, became a magnet for thousands of immigrants. Upon arrival, Italians took up any available occupation to earn a livelihood. They were ragpickers, refuse sorters, and, until the Greeks arrived and became competitors, the leading pushcart fruit sellers. And despite the outward drudgery and griminess of the job, Italians excelled as bootblacks. They were also successful as barbers and tailors.

As in New York, people grouped together with compatriots from Italy, maintaining Old World ties and keeping European traditions alive. The Philadelphia Italian community was enlivened by

LEFT: *Street musicians entertain outside a store in Philadelphia's Italian Market. Located on 9th Street in South Philly, it is the largest outdoor food market in the world.*

its many social clubs, such as Palumbo's on Catherine Street, and other businesses such as restaurants and grocery stores that specialized in Italian products (salami, pepperoni, cheese, wine, garlic, and olive oil) in order to satisfy the demand for familiar products. Today, South Philadelphia's Italian market, on 9th Street, is the world's largest outdoor food market. Many families have been running the same stores for the past 125 years, and the market is still well-known for the high quality of the food sold.

ABOVE: *Wherever Italian immigrants settled, they established food markets for the fresh fruits and vegetables they needed.*

RIGHT: *Fresh fish on sale at a stall in Philadelphia's Italian Market. The Italians are passionate about the quality their of food.*

ITALIANS OF NEW JERSEY

In the 1880s, the number of southern Italians residing in New York City soon overflowed and as a result many made their way to the neighboring state of New Jersey, where men found seasonal work in the cranberry bogs and in the orchards (some of these workers came from other cities, working seasonally on fruit farms and returning to their permanent residence at the end of the job).

Soon small Little Italies blossomed in other places like Newark, Jersey City, Hoboken, and Paterson.

Hoboken is where Pietro di Donato's famous novel *Christ in Concrete* is set which was the story that inspired Jimmy Breslin to write *The Short Sweet Dream of Eduardo Gutierrez*. Donato's novel is based on the real-life events of Good Friday 1923, when his father—a construction worker—fell to his death at a construction site. Donato was only 12 years old at the time, and his published book became a

cult novel because of its instant success and its appeal for many immigrant families. It became the protest novel for their generation.

Because of its agricultural benefits, the Garden State was a major attraction to Italian Americans who had been used to farming in the old country. It was in New Jersey, in 1878, that Secchi de Casale founded the farming community of Vineland. De Casale was one of the followers of the revolutionary Giuseppe Mazzini, who had been forced to flee to America after the collapse of the ill-fated Roman Republic in 1849. In New York, de Casale founded America's first Italian language newspaper, *L'Eco d'Italia*, and thereafter devoted much of his time to offering guidance and aid to Italians entering the country. Concerned about the unwholesome life in the city slums, de Casale sought ways to divert the stream of immigrants to rural districts. With the aid of American landowner Charles Landis, de Casale established an agricultural colony where Italians produced grapes and marketed wine. They also found success with crops of beans, sweet potatoes, tomatoes, and peaches. By 1905, more than 6,000 Italians were working in Vineland and others had settled in nearby villages.

LEFT: *This Vineland farm was established by Italian immigrants in 1878, and it has managed to continue its operation up to the present day.*

ABOVE RIGHT: *A statue of Saint Joseph is paraded through the streets of Boston's Little Italy during a festival, one of many happening across the country.*

ITALIANS OF BOSTON

The North End of Boston had seen successive waves of immigrants since the 1700s, but from the 1870s and the 1880s, Italians dominated the neighborhood. In 1873 Italians founded St. Leonard's Church, the spiritual center of Boston's Little Italy. By 1920 the North End was 90 percent Italian. Like other Italian communities, it was close-knit, with an Old World atmosphere. They worked as day laborers, bootblacks, pushcart hawkers, fishermen, and shopkeepers; others worked in distilleries and molasses factories. Despite the fact that the Italian community suffered greatly during the 1920s trial and execution of Nicola Sacco and Bartolomeo Vanzetti (*see pages 72–73*), the North End has retained its vibrancy. With its seveteenth century layout of narrow winding streets and its many cafés and Italian delis, it still evokes the atmosphere of the nineteenth century.

ITALIANS OF CHICAGO

Railroad connections made Chicago the cross-roads of America, and immigrants from Genoa and Lucca, in northern Italy began settling there as early as the 1850s. Rarely employed in factories, Chicago Italians found jobs as railroad and construction laborers, shoemakers, barbers, and inevitably as fruit and vegetable peddlers; others came to work in the stockyards, slaughterhouses, and meatpacking plants, or bustled off to other parts of Illinois and the Midwest. Some became saloonkeepers, confectioners, and makers of plaster statuettes. The explosion of southern Italian immigration in the 1880s established the first large Italian colony in the city's Near North Side district, which became known as Little Sicily. In this predominantly slum neighborhood, the Italian population reached 20,000 by 1920.

One of the most famous (supposedly haunted) settlement houses in this district was Hull House. Set up by Jane Addams and a college friend in 1889, the house became a beacon for the growing number of destitute people in the Near West Side area of Chicago. The house was a shelter for immigrant communities as well as the city's poor and uneducated. Jane Addams was hailed as one of the important social reformers of the time as a result of her efforts on behalf of the underprivileged.

Perhaps the most famous Chicago Italian was the notorious gangster Al Capone (*see page 76*), who

RIGHT: *Although many of Chicago's Little Italies were razed during construction projects in the 1960s, Taylor Street is still a vibrant community, and its Italian markets sell the finest produce.*

also won a sort of popularity as a modern "Robin Hood" because of his legendary generosity toward the city's homeless and poverty stricken. Also well-known for this cause is Mother Cabrini (*see pages 116–117*), who died in Chicago in 1917 after a lifetime dedicated to helping the less fortunate.

Following World War II, the Little Italies of Chicago were broken up by successive programs aimed at transportation improvement. These projects saw the creation of highways and railroads running through former Italian neighborhoods. Construction of the University of Illinois also razed Italian settlements to make room for academia, but Taylor Street still boasts some wonderful Italian restaurants, cafés, and shops.

ITALIANS OF NEW ORLEANS

New Orleans was one of the biggest ports in the southern states, and it attracted Italian immigrants as early as 1840. The city was a true melting pot, having received many successive waves of immigrants over the years, and the Italians were the last ethnic group to settle here.

Many came to work in the cotton fields and in the Central American fruit importing trade. Some Italians who entered through the port of New Orleans stayed only briefly, residing in the French Quarter, before continuing to places like Bryan, Texas, or the agricultural community of Tonitown, Arkansas, both of which also had thriving Italian communities. Others stayed on to establish a neighborhood that came to be known as Little Palermo, because of the Sicilians living there.

By 1890 about 15,000 ethnic Italians lived in the city, 93 percent of whom were Sicilian. This was the biggest Sicilian population outside Sicily, and the second largest center of Italian immigrants in the United States, after New York City.

Despite violent riots against the Italian community at the end of the nineteenth century (*see pages 72–73*), Italians soon made their mark on this city. As they did in other Little Italies across the country, they became involved in the food industry, opening stores and delis to sell familiar products. It is to Italian immigrants that New Orleans owes its famous *muffaletta* sandwich, one of the gourmet city's prime treats.

RIGHT: *New Orleans' Italian community, predominantly Sicilian in origin, grew to become the second largest in the United States, after New York's.*

ITALIANS OF SAN FRANCISCO

San Francisco's Italian community had a different character compared to other large American cities because its first influx of immigrants came from northern Italy. The gold rush attracted many Genoans to the West, and they first settled in the business district before moving to Telegraph Hill after 1870. Later they established themselves in North Beach and Russian Hill, where they were joined by increasing numbers of Sicilians.

Many Genoans joined the fishing fleets, first working on boats, then buying and operating their own. Later they became prominent in the canning industry as well. Baseball great Joe DiMaggio was the son of an Italian fisherman in San Francisco.

Good farmland also attracted Italians to northern California. The age-old tradition of winemaking was a natural for Italian entrepreneurs, and they established many of the state's leading wineries. In 1881, Andrea Sbarbaro founded the Italian-Swiss Colony winery in Sonoma County, while the Napa Valley soon boasted the Sebastiani and Martini winery. In the Central Valley, the Petri and Cribari wineries have flourished alongside the famous Ernest and Julio Gallo winery, which dates from 1933.

ABOVE: *Italian immigrants, like the Gallo brothers, established many of California's leading wineries.*

BELOW: *The first Italian immigrants made their way out west from the late 1840s, attracted by the money to be made during the Gold Rush.*

ABOVE: *In the early decades of the twentieth century, San Francisco's Fisherman's Wharf bustled daily as hundreds of Italian fishermen landed their catches.*

RIGHT: *Baseball superstar Joe DiMaggio, the son of a Genoese fisherman, opened a seafood restaurant on Fisherman's Wharf in the 1940s.*

Italian farmers required financial support, and one of their compatriots filled that need. In 1904, A. P. Giannini (1870–1949) founded the Bank of Italy in San Francisco to serve Italian farmers who couldn't obtain loans from other banks. The son of Genoese immigrants (his father was a farmer in San Jose), Giannini made enough money in the produce business so that by the time he was in his thirties, he could have retired. But having seen that no financial institution would support Italian Americans who were trying to make their way in agriculture, he was determined to fill the gap. He was immediately successful, lending to small immigrant and first-generation businessmen. After the great earthquake and fire that devastated San Francisco in 1906, Giannini was the only banker

ABOVE: *The San Francisco earthquake inspired national sympathy. Here, New Yorkers collect clothing to donate to earthquake victims.*

who would make immediate loans to businessmen trying to rebuild. With about $2 million, which he had salvaged from the rubble of his bank, he set up a stall and lent money to people he knew either personally or by reputation, trusting them to pay him back in time. By the 1920s, under the name of the Bank of America, his bank had grown into the third largest bank in the country, and at the time of his death in 1949, the Bank of America was the country's largest.

LEFT: *Many Italians prospered as farmers in California, where climate and conditions suited agriculture.*

RIGHT: *Ghirardelli Square, located around the site of the Ghirardelli's first chocolate factory, is now a thriving tourist attraction.*

One of the earliest Italian success stories was that of Domenico Ghirardelli (1817–1894), who landed San Francisco in 1849. The son of a chocolate maker in Rapallo, Italy, he founded his famous factory in 1856. He was so successful that he and his sons soon expanded the business, buying a defunct woolen mill, which they enlarged and renovated to serve as his new factory. Over the years he added to it until he had created a complex that encompassed an entire city block and even included subsidized housing for his workers. The area around it was eventually named Ghirardelli Square and is now a major tourist attraction. When the factory moved to San Leandro in the 1960s, the premises were renovated to house stores, as well as a display of antique chocolate-making machinery.

STRUGGLES

POVERTY

Italians quickly found themselves at a disadvantage in the New World, for it seemed that one needed money to do anything worthwhile: money to travel from town to town; money to go out West; money to set up a stores, buy land, or buy a house; and money to send home to the family in Italy. Yet the expense of the ocean crossing had left them barely enough to satisfy the immigration inspectors at Ellis Island. In fact, the journey was often financed by a *padrone* or a relative, and so the immi-

> ### OLD ITALIAN SAYING
>
> *"Well, I came to America because I heard the streets were paved with gold. When I got here I found out three things: first, the streets weren't paved with gold; second, they weren't paved at all; and third, I was expected to pave them."*

grant was in debt upon arrival. On top of this, Italians felt they had been completely misinformed about the conditions they would have to endure to earn a wage in the United States.

LEFT: *Although wages were higher than in Italy, Italian immigrants were among the lowest paid workers in the United States.*

ABOVE: *In the 1920s, work was scarce for all, so President Roosevelt set up the Works Progress Administration to create jobs.*

Many found themselves stuck in slums where life was shadowy, dirty, and grim; such an existence left them feeling empty, despairing, and frustrated. As poor as Italy was, at least it was beautiful, bright, and sunny, with a sense of space. In contrast, slum life typically involved living in a tenement house—commonly a tall building of five floors housing 100

or so residents. On the whole, only one-third of New York City's tenements had running water, and in most cases privacy was a dream. In 1893, 12,434 persons lived in the Italian slum on Centre Street, in Lower Manhattan, where apartments rented for $4.60 per month. Problems with cleanliness and sanitation made life precarious in such places. By 1900 there were thousands of tenements, flop-houses, and other inferior dwellings for immigrants on the Lower East Side, on the Upper East Side, in Harlem, and in other cities like Rochester, Buffalo, and Newark. In the 1880s a street called Mulberry Bend in New York's Little Italy was decidedly the worst of the Italian slums: it seemed to epitomize sordidness, misery, crime, and disease (*see page 70*).

To make matters worse, Italians were among the lowest paid laborers in America (sometimes receiving as little as 30 cents a day) and were compelled to work long, grueling hours doing backbreaking labor. The only day of rest for them was Sunday. Yet wages were still higher here than in Italy, and so this dilemma made many "birds of passage" reconsider the original plan to send large amounts of money back to Italy. If pay was higher here, then there was an economic advantage in bringing the whole family to America. The situation in America was far from perfect, but the Catholic Church, the Italian language press, immigrant banks, mutual aid societies, and a rich cultural life in the "colony" all served to give them confidence and fostered in them a growing sense of security.

THE CATHOLIC CHURCH AND MUTUAL AID

The Italians' faith in the Catholic Church was never more important than in a time of need. However, their strong belief in tradition set them apart from other cultures living in America making it harder for them to be accepted. To the dismay of the Italians, Catholicism in the United States was almost completely dominated by an Irish hierarchy, with the parishes largely run by Irish priests. These Irish priests found the southern Italians' and Sicilians' passionate and expressive devotion to the Virgin Mary and the holy saints (as seen in public processions and worship) distasteful, especially when it attracted the attention of Protestants, which only served to create more hostility.

This stressful situation heightened the vast cultural divide that separated the Italians not only from the Irish but from other newcomers as well (such as the Poles, Slovaks, and Portuguese). It was only through the intercession of the Pope in 1893 that steps were eventually taken to aid the Italians by organizing the San Raffaele Society (or the Italian Immigration Society as it was known on Ellis Island) in New York for the protection of immigrants. The Reverend Father Gaspare Moretto served as its chaplain and director for nearly 30 years, and his work on Ellis Island and in Little Italy did much to ease the distress. In a 1910 Christmas address to detained Italians he said:

"I have spoken at Ellis Island before, but never was there a time when I felt so bad as now. There are so many detained here. You have crossed the ocean, endured hardships and danger to come to the country discovered by your fellow countryman. You have found the door closed. You have had your hope in the land of liberty shattered. To those who will finally get in, I would say, you must live to be a credit to your country and the land of your adoption."

In addition to the Catholic Church, other groups also offered help. The Scalabrinian Missionaries were founded by Bishop John Baptist Scalabrini in 1887 specifically for Italian immigrants, and later Order of the Sons of Italy was founded in New York (1905)—an organization that grew phenomenally, with 125,000 members and 887 lodges throughout the country by 1921. Other aid societies that immigrants joined included the Societa Italiana di Mutua Beneficenza in San Francisco, the Italian Welfare League in New York, and the Societa di Mutuo Soccorso in Chicago.

LEFT: *Crowding at Ellis Island, as seen here in a picture from 1920, could make conditions for detained immigrants very unpleasant, and representatives from the Catholic Church did all they could to make things easier.*

LLITERACY PROBLEMS

Illiteracy and resistance to change were major issues for the new immigrants. This was hardly surprising, as southern Italy had one of the highest illiteracy rates in Europe. Many adults lacked an education and saw no reason why their children should be any different. Many parents also resisted change because they were, quite frankly, suspicious of Americans and were shocked at the casualness and laxity of American families where children often questioned their parents' authority and roamed the streets as they chose. There was also fear that if the children learned English, they would cease to be Italians; for this reason many fathers and mothers sent their offspring only to Italian schools run by the Catholic Church, which placed a far greater value on keeping families united, Catholic, and wholly Italian. It was not until the 1920s that southern Italian immigrants began to recognize the importance of an adequate education if they were to succeed in America. Aside from this, the great barrier that delayed success was language.

LEFT: *Many Italian immigrants were devout Catholics, raising their children within the church. This picture,* Confirmation Class, *by Fannie Eliza Duvall (1897) shows girls preparing for the important ceremony.*

LANGUAGE BARRIERS AND THE RISE OF ITALGLISH

Because so many southern Italians came to the United States as temporary workers, there was a reluctance to become better acquainted with English; there was often no pressing need to learn the language because they could rely on the experienced *padroni*—Italians with greater linguistic facility—or the permanent settlers in Italian neighborhoods. Even so, newcomers soon learned that the Italian language known at home was spoken differently by Italians themselves, depending on the region in Italy where they had been brought up. This was a shock, as encountering so many types of Italians emphasized the numerous real differences among Italians themselves. Their dialects varied so drastically (especially from North to South, and between Sicily and the peninsula) they had great difficulty understanding each other.

FROM A POLITICAL SPEECH DELIVERED IN MIXED NEAPOLITAN TO A CROWD OF ITALIANS IN BOSTON, 1909

"La carta serve a tante e tante cose: puo ave'na giobba in corte, o fa o polisse." (Citizenship papers are useful for so many things: you can get a job in court or become a policeman.)

LEFT: *Mulberry Bend, in New York City's Little Italy, was notorious as the worst of Italian slums.*

Sardinians presented yet another problem, for many of them did not even speak Italian. Their language, Sardinian (like French, Spanish, and Portuguese), was a direct offspring of Latin, with its own grammar, vocabulary, and dialects—quite separate from Italian. As for Sicilian, at times it seemed to be a language different from Italian in spite of the fact that it was only a regional variation. Because immigrants came from places as diverse as Puglia, Romagna, Molise, Lucca, the Abruzzi, and Umbria, they sought to overcome the linguistic barriers by using expressions that they could all understand from more widely known dialects, or by using an idiom of their own invention: Italglish.

Italglish was especially useful because it helped Italians cope with their new American environment, one that seemed radically strange to them: tall buildings, subway trains, crowds of people rushing about, and chattering away in loud voices in a language that was utterly incomprehensible. This environment introduced them to English words, many of them unpronounceable. But

---

SOME ITALGLISH WORDS

Arriope!: Hurry up!

Auschieppe: Housekeeper

Azzollo: That's all

Azzo rait: That's all right

Boifrendo: Boyfriend

Ciunga: Chewing gum

Dringo: Drink

Fare u stingio: To be a cheapskate

Farmaiolo: Farmer

Fruttistene: Fruit stand

Ghenga: Gang

Grignollo: Greenhorn, newcomer

Il Forte Gelato: Fourth of July

Sannemogogna: Son of a gun

Uat sa ius?: What's the use?

---

the Italians were game, and extremely resourceful.

This immigrant idiom flourished between 1870 and 1950, primarily among greenhorns, in Italian families, and in Little Italies, and finally among elderly immigrants. At its height it was widely used in the immigrant press (as shown in the sentence taken from a speech delivered in 1909 on *page 70*) and it was still heard in Italian language radio programs of the 1930s and 1940s.

BELOW: *A young Italian boy does his English homework in his tenement apartment. Often only the children learned English, while their parents got by with Italian or Italglish.*

71

AMERICAN PREJUDICE

The American reaction to southern Italian immigrants was often openly negative and hostile. An Italian was commonly referred to derisively as a "macaroni," "spaghetti," "dago," or "wop." These terms were even used in widely respected publications such as *Harper's Weekly* and the *New York Times*, as well as in minor publications like *Everybody's Magazine*, which published a story about Italians in 1911 entitled "Just Wops." In addition, southern Italians were constantly reviled as volatile, lawless, dishonest, dangerous, and criminally inclined. Some of the country's leading newspapers regularly published articles and stories that sought to spread fear of southern Italians and Sicilians. Most especially the stories focused on the Mafia and other organizations—such as the Camorra (of Naples) and the Black Hand (La Mano Nera).

It is this kind of climate that explains the tragedy and prejudice behind the famous Sacco and Vanzetti trial. In 1920 a paymaster was robbed and killed by two men; the Bridgewater, Massachusetts, chief of police linked a similar robbery in the area to this crime, and found the perfect culprits in two Italian immigrants. One thing led to another, Sacco

ABOVE: *Prejudice comes in many forms. Often immigrants who had been in the United States for long enough to become very Americanized were the most hostile to greenhorns.*

BELOW: *Anti-Italian prejudice was even expressed in popular music, as shown by this musical cover sheet denigrating Italian Americans*

Shall **Capitalists** MURDER Our Fighters!

you shall BURN Our Figh

Sacco -&- Vanzetti Em

A PROTES' STRIK!

BOYCOTT MASSACHUSETTS PRODUCTS

Can Save Our Martyrs!

LEFT: *In August, 1927, more than 12,000 gathered in Union Square in New York City to protest against the guilty verdict in the Sacco and Vanzetti trial.*

BELOW: *Sacco and Vanzetti, seen here with a prison guard, were condemned to death following an unjust trial. Many believed that they were framed because of anti-Italian prejudice.*

and Vanzetti were imprisoned, and then they were put on trial for another crime—the South Braintree murders. Despite evidence delivered from eyewitnesses and reactions ignited worldwide against the unfair trial these two men received, they were caught in a trap. Judge Webster Thayer repeatedly denied a new trial, letting his obvious bias surface throughout the inquest. In 1927, Sacco and Vanzetti were executed by electrocution. Although the truth was never determined either way, their case stands out in history as an example of how prejudice can poison legal procedures and cost innocent lives.

ORGANIZED CRIME

With early roots in Italian history, secret criminal leagues began as political organizations supporting the rights of oppressed peasants against government officials wielding power stemming from faraway governments. Between 1880 and 1920, some members of organized criminal groups sensed that there would be new opportunities for them in America, and they joined the waves of immigrants sailing across the Atlantic. They settled in the Little Italies that were growing in many American cities and continued their illicit activities. The Black Hand, for instance, was notorious for extorting "protection" money from Italian immigrants, especially those running small businesses.

Organized crime established its first foothold in the United States in New Orleans in the 1880s. It was perceived as a serious enough threat to public order to warrant a dedicated police investigation led by the city's police commissioner, David C. Hennessy. However, before he could

NEW YORK DAILY TRIBUNE

On March 23, 1891, the following words
appeared in a published article:

*"Italian citizens of the United States . . .
are not in doubt of the fact that not only
in New Orleans but in . . . large cities
throughout the country Italians of
criminal antecedents and propensities . . .
are closely affiliated for the purpose of
requiting injuries and gratifying
animosities by secret vengeance. These
organizations . . . are connected with the
Mafia. Through their agency the most
infernal crimes have been committed . . .
They have succeeded in keeping their
existence and doings wrapped in
mystery and darkness."*

make the findings of his investigation public, he
was murdered, allegedly by the Mafia. Numerous
Italians were arrested as suspects and then released;
at one point as many as 40 were being held simul-
taneously. Finally, nine newly arrived Sicilians were
singled out as the most likely suspects and charged
as principals in the murder; seven others were
named accessories to the crime. They were also
accused of being members of the Mafia. However,
when tried before judge and jury, they were found
not guilty. Despite the court's findings, an enraged
mob took the law into their own hands, storming
the jail, lynching two of the suspects, and gunning
down nine others in the parish prison yard. This
was the largest single lynching in U.S. history and
one of the worst anti-immigrant assaults in Louisiana.

This event provoked a good deal of public
debate about secret societies like the Mafia.

LEFT: *Al Capone attracted some
powerful enemies in Chicago,
including this group, shown
after their arrest [left to right]:
Michael Bizarro, Joseph Aiello,
Joseph Rubinello, Jack
Monzello, and Joseph Russio.*

RIGHT: *Some of the leading figures
in Italian organized crime, from
left, Vito Genovese, Charles
"Lucky" Luciano, and lastly,
Joseph Profaci.*

LEFT: *Al Capone, the Chicago crime boss, was one of the most flamboyant gangsters of the Prohibition era.*

BELOW: *During the Depression, Capone funded a soup kitchen, giving free food to the city's poor and paying for it out of the proceeds of organized crime.*

Afterward, whenever a southern Italian was involved in a criminal case, the question of association with the Mafia predictably arose. For some reason, the press preferred to ignore the fact that less than 1 percent of southern Italian immigrants were involved in crime.

In the 1920s, the public's fear was mingled with admiration as organized crime assumed a higher profile during Prohibition. A few Italian Americans made fortunes in bootlegging, racketeering, and prostitution, displaying their wealth in public, enjoying an ostentatious lifestyle and almost courting media attention. Attention was focused on criminals such as the flamboyant bootleg racketeer Al Capone in Chicago, who claimed to have made $105 million from his criminal activities in 1927, only two years before the stock market crash that

FREE SOUP

ushered in the Great Depression. In fact, during the Depression he used his millions to help fellow residents in Chicago, running Free Soup kitchen, and making many charitable donations.

Italian-born Charles "Lucky" Luciano (1897–1962) also attracted attention because of his lavish spending habits—he wore the finest clothes and lived in a suite in New York City's Waldorf-Astoria Hotel. His alliance with Jewish criminal mastermind Meyer Lansky helped him to restructure organized crime and led to the creation of Murder, Inc., a national crime syndicate. These and other criminals were romanticized in Hollywood films such as *Scarface*, with Paul Muni and George Raft (himself half-Italian), and *Little Caesar* and *Key Largo*, with Edward G. Robinson.

But the heyday of organized crime was short-lived: By 1933 Capone, Luciano, and other criminal masterminds were in jail or had gone out of business. Capone was imprisoned on tax evasion charges (despite the many murders for which he was responsible). Luciano was jailed after convictions for pimping, but after helping the American government during World War II, he secured early release and was deported to Italy, where he died in 1962, lonely and homesick for the United States.

ABOVE: *Hollywood films, such as Scarface (1932), glamorized the criminal underworld.*

BELOW: *Lucky Luciano [center] is escorted into court by two detectives in 1936 to face charges of pimping.*

NOT LONG BEFORE HE DIED, LUCKY LUCIANO WAS ASKED IF HE'D DO ANYTHING DIFFERENTLY IF HE COULD.

This was his reply: "I'd do it legal. I learned too late that you need just as good a brain to make a crooked million as an honest million. These days you apply for a license to steal from the public. If I had my time again, I'd make sure I got that license first."

BECOMING ITALIAN AMERICAN

THE ASSIMILATION OF ITALIANS

Many traditional Italian families underwent a drastic metamorphosis when they moved to America. The old ways, which viewed the father as undisputed master of the household, were slowly broken down because of the difficulty the parents had in communicating in English. Children tended to learn the language more quickly and efficiently than their parents and this gave them a voice in family decision-making that they never would have had in Italy. Many boys took advantage of this situation and, because they were sent out to work, had even more opportunities to put their newly found influence to use.

The new ways also changed the lives of Italian girls, who were no longer kept at home as before but also were sent out to work. By 1919 an astonishing 91 percent of Italian girls above the age of 14 were wage earners in New York City.

All this change and development weakened parental control, and eventually many young Italians—particularly young men—broke away entirely from their families and branched out on their own. In this new life, many of them left the old ethnic neighborhoods, selected their own wives, and adopted American ways. Most young Italians realized that assimilation largely meant conforming to American society, but they didn't abandon their ancestry completely. They often maintained the most cherished ways of old Italy, incorporating them into their new lives as a strong link between past and present .

The role of schools

Although a number of organizations helped to assimilate Italians, the most powerful influence was the public school system. In a very real sense, schools were the nation's key instruments for introducing foreigners to the English language, and to the values and norms of Anglo-American culture. They taught them what was acceptable and what was not. Schoolteachers and administrators compelled immigrants to conform to these standards of behavior and discipline, which peasant families were quite unacquainted with. Schools also introduced immigrants to patriotic songs, recitation of the Pledge of Allegiance, and respect for the Declaration of Independence, the Constitution, and the Founding Fathers, especially George Washington. The first names of pupils even underwent occasional modification as teachers started calling them Joan or Jane instead of Giovanna, or Joseph instead of Giuseppe.

ABOVE: Not all children benefited from free education in America. Some, like this ten-year-old boy, had to work in the factories to help support their families.

RIGHT: The children of immigrants study English in their classroom at the Essex Market School on New York City's Lower East Side in 1894.

ABOVE: *Hull House, founded by Jane Addams, was the best-known settlement house in Chicago.*

The role of settlement houses

Settlement houses were also helpful to the newcomers as places where they could learn English, American history and government, music, painting, sculpting, athletic activities, and games. Field trips introduced immigrants to museums and to the delights of the American countryside. Many settlement houses also had libraries and reading rooms for members. The Henry Street Settlement in New York and Hull House in Chicago (*see page 60*) were among the best-known settlement houses in the country.

The Young Men's Christian Association and the North American Civic League for Immigrants were foremost in the Americanization movement, teach-ing immigrants American values and patriotism. They persuaded public schools to open night classes in foreign neighborhoods, for instruction in English, American civics, and history, in prepara-tion for future citizenship. Such groups also printed leaflets for American citizens on the effects of immigration and advocated ways to help foreign-ers adapt to American life.

New identity in a new land: Name changing

The chance to change one's identity was an oppor-tunity that some immigrants could not resist. Most Europeans who came from the lower levels of a rigid society simply could not alter their occupa-tion or way of life without arousing suspicion; these were limits and constraints that one simply had to live with. But in America, a new way of life was possible, and every immigrant seemed to know it—if not at the Italian dock, then at least once aboard the steerage deck and breathing in the salty air of the open sea. And one way of starting afresh was to change one's name.

Italians changed their names to conform to American customs and to avoid being discriminat-ed against or insulted and also to symbolize a new start. For most people, the solution was simply to modify the spelling of a difficult name. Thus Buono became Bono, and Desimone became Desmond; Amici turned into Ameche, Bartolomeo was dropped in favor of Bartolo, and Viscogliosi was transformed into Visco. Some went further by changing their names to the English equivalent: Bianco became White, Piccolo turned into Little, and Fiori became Flowers; others simply dropped Italian apostrophes, so that D'Amore became Damore, and D'Angelo became Dangelo. Employers also influenced name changes because many clerks misspelled foreign names, and foremen mispronounced them or dispensed with them entirely, calling an immigrant something else. So Giacoso became Jock, Rossi was transformed into Ross, and Benedetto became Bennett.

SOCIOLOGIST MICHAEL LA SORTE HAS EFFECTIVELY DISMISSED THE CLAIM THAT INSPECTORS WERE RESPONSIBLE FOR DICTATING NAMES

"The popular belief that new names were handed out . . . at Ellis Island, or that the ignorant . . . powerless immigrant had no choice but to succumb to a permanent name change . . . clouds the more obvious and less [appealing] explanation [that] name changing was an adaptive concession that some immigrants chose to make to their new environment."

One persistent myth that has spread in recent years is the spurious claim that immigrants' names were deliberately changed at Ellis Island as routine policy; no motive other than capriciousness is offered to support this. If an inspector had ever done such a thing, he would usually have done it on the sly. The prime reason why names were changed was because immigrants were given no official identity cards when released from Ellis Island, and so once off the island, they were free to call themselves by whatever name they fancied.

BELOW: *Children from New York City's Henry Street Settlement gather before being sent off to a summer camp in the woods to enjoy a two-week vacation out of the city.*

Marrying non-Italians

Although members of the immigrant generation tended to marry other Italians, their offspring increasingly wed those of other nationalities, although this was truer of sons than of daughters. Their preference was to marry other Catholics, especially Irish, Germans, French, Poles, or Lithuanians, although some married English, Scottish, or Swedish Protestants and other immigrant offspring married Jews. Over the decades, the number marrying non-Italians increased considerably, as is shown by the outmarriage rate among the Italians of Buffalo, which rose from 12 percent in 1930 to 27 percent in 1950 to 50 percent in 1960. By 1990 the outmarriage rate for Italians nationwide had reached 60 percent.

THE PULL OF ITALY: MUSSOLINI AND THE RISE OF FASCISM

The rise of Benito Mussolini to power in Italy in the 1920s created an outpouring of excitement and pride in Italy, which, through his government, became a serious player in European affairs. He was widely praised in the American press for disciplining the nation and the spirit of Mussolini's fascism quickly spread to Italian-American communities and enthralled thousands, including congressman Fiorello LaGuardia. This enthusiasm increased tremendously with the Lateran Treaty in early 1929 (recognizing the Vatican as an independent sovereign state), when

General Balbo (Minister of Air Forces) flew 25 Savoia-Marchetti flying boats from Italy to the Chicago World's Fair in 1933 as a show of Italian aeronautical skill, and when Mussolini conquered Ethiopia in 1935. Italian-American support for *Il Duce* began to weaken only after he joined Germany in the invasion of France in June 1940.

RIGHT: Mussolini lost many Italian-American supporters when he allied with Germany during World War II.

BELOW: Carrying the flags of the fascist legions, the Italian army in a rally in Rome in 1936

Enemy aliens

World War II was an especially difficult time for Italian Americans, and the military alliance of Italy, Germany, and Japan caused much heartache for those who had emigrated from these countries. The U.S. government was also concerned: When World War II broke out in September 1939, following Germany's invasion of Poland, President Franklin D. Roosevelt ordered J. Edgar Hoover, the director of the Federal Bureau of Investigation (FBI), to compile a list of potentially dangerous Germans, Italians, and Japanese. In 1940 Congress passed the Alien Registration Act, requiring all noncitizens to register. After the Japanese attack on Pearl Harbor on December 7, 1941, which brought the United States into the war, Japanese, German, and Italian alien suspects were arrested by the FBI. By June 1942 more than 1,500 Italians had been apprehended, 264 of whom were interned. One of those arrested by the FBI was the famed opera singer Ezio Pinza, who told his story several years later in his memoirs.

The accusations against Pinza were that he possessed a ring with a Nazi swastika on it; he owned a boat equipped with a radio that received and sent secret messages; he was a personal friend of Benito

"On Thursday, March 12, 1942, at 11 o'clock in the morning, two well-dressed young men entered my house through the back door without ringing the bell. The two came straight up to me.

'Are you Ezio Pinza?' one of them asked me sharply.

'Yes, I am. What can I do for you?'

'In the name of the President of the United States, you are under arrest.'"

LEFT: *Opera singer Ezio Pinza shown after his release from detention; he was arrested by the FBI on suspicion of being an active supporter of Mussolini's fascist regime.*

Mussolini; and he sent secret coded messages through changes in the tempo of his voice while singing over the radio each Saturday. After two hearings, a further investigation based on his denials, and numerous testimonials concerning his character, the accusations were proved false. Pinza was finally released on June 4, 1942, although most other Italians were not freed until after Italy surrendered on September 8, 1943. One vestige of this era can be found on the wall of a detention room on Ellis Island, that reads *Viva Mussolini!*

Patriots

World War II was a time when Italian Americans demonstrated their patriotism in unprecedented numbers. Of the 12 million men under arms,

1 million of them were of Italian heritage. Strangely, a mixture of their experience at this time, patriotism combined with ethnic prejudice, came to symbolize the core of the Italian-American immigrant plight in general. So while many were fighting for America, whole communities of Italians living along the California coast—in enclaves where they had settled as fishermen, storekeepers, and farm and factory workers—were evacuated. The "enemy aliens" were removed and ordered to live inland. But the war did give Italians a chance to show their loyalty, even at the expense of fighting Italy. Among the notable heroes were John Basilone, the first enlisted man to receive the Medal of Honor, and Don Gentile, America's first combat ace described as our "one man air force" by General Eisenhower.

BELOW: *Italian prisoners of war were held in prison camps in the United States. Many individuals were treated with suspicion or accused of treason.*

RIGHT: *Flying Ace Don Gentile [top row, far right] made a heroic contribution to the war effort during World War II.*

ABOVE: *School was an ideal place for children to mix with those from different countries—this helped them adapt to their new environment.*

RIGHT: *When the immigrants first arrived, the priority was for the men to find work to support themselves and to help their families.*

THE ITALIAN AMERICAN WAY

CHANGE AND ADAPTATION

Italian Americans would always cherish the customs and traditions of their immigrant forefathers, but over the years many of these customs underwent various changes because of the new American environment. For example, a traditional Italian recipe calling for an unavailable ingredient would have to be made with an American substitute. Similarly, a certain religious *festa* might omit particular preparations that in a small Italian village would have been essential but in an American city seemed less so. These and other modifications created a distinctive Italian-American culture, with gradual emergence of "the American" character as interpreted in literature, films, and paintings through Italian eyes.

As mentioned earlier in the section on Italglish, Italian expressions started to be intermixed with American slang and English idiomatic phases, proving that the immigrants were adapting and becoming part of America. More than anything, the loss of *la bella lingua*—with its apt expressions and its exquisite melody—as the primary means of communication represented the final change from the old ways to the new. The substitution of English for Italian was a defining mark in the immi-

BELOW: *Immigrants had to become accustomed to different foods available in the market, as part of the process of assimilation.*

grant transition. This, along with the gradual loss of the old immigrant generation—the disappearance of the Italian-born *nonno* and *nonna* (grandpa and grandma)—has been painful indeed, for the real connection between generations lay in the closeness of the Italian family.

La famiglia: The Italian-American family

For Italian Americans, the family has always been more important than the individual: A person is only a branch, whereas the family is the root. Tradition held that personal action only mattered in relation to the honor or dishonor it brought to the household. So from this standpoint, wrongdoing was serious only when it besmirched and disgraced the family name.

The tradition of male authority within the family was sacrosanct to Italians and was sustained in Italian-American families for a long time after they settled in the United States. Sanctioned by the moral authority of the Roman Catholic Church, it provided clear-cut roles for husbands, wives, and children and remained unvarying down through generations. This arrangement fostered a remarkably stable family structure, which made Italians the envy of many Americans. To Italians, the chief object of marriage was to have children and instruct them in the same ways so that they too could play the same roles in the generation to follow. Thus large families were esteemed—and not only among rural people. Although the man was recognized as the ultimate source of authority in the family and wives were required to be submissive, this by no means prevented a woman from exercising considerable power behind the scenes.

The roles of children were also determined by gender. Sons were expected to work outside the home, often with their fathers or other males; in this way, they learned to become breadwinners, against the day when they would have their own wives and children to care for. At home, sons were put on a higher level than daughters, and their sisters were expected to clean their clothes, cook for them, and the like—all of which was considered "women's work." As adolescents, sons were allowed more freedom outside the home, whereas girls were expected to perform household chores in preparation for the day when they would become wives. Needless to say, these ideal Italian family customs underwent a drastic change in America. Families became considerably smaller, and fathers were no longer the *paterfamilias* of old. Sons and daughters are now more equal than before, and both can look forward to a college education and to selecting their own spouses.

LEFT: *Mealtimes were always an important occasion for Italian families. They were a chance for everyone to be together.*

BELOW: *Traditionally, women were expected to stay at home while the men went out to work.*

ABOVE: *Gradually, the family emphasis would change, so that Italian sons and daughters became more equal in their livestyles in the United States.*

FOOD

When Italian immigrants arrived in the New World, they were unable to find many of the ingredients they were accustomed to using in everyday meals—sweet, ripe tomatoes; fresh herbs; arborio rice. At the same time, meat, like other food, was abundant and far cheaper than it had been in Italy, which was a welcome delight. Around the turn of the century, the average Italian family spent about three-quarters of its income on food, but in America this decreased to one-quarter.

Adaptation to different conditions and availabilities gave rise to a new cuisine—an Italian-American one. Instead of relying on the natural sweetness of ripe tomatoes, Italian-American cooks enhanced the taste of poorer fresh tomatoes (or even canned ones) by adding garlic, sweet onions, a pinch of sugar, and lots of dried herbs. They could afford to use lots of meat, for example, in making the large meatballs that are the hallmark of "spaghetti and meatballs" served around the country today. (In Italy, *polpette* are smaller, flatter, and generally served without sauce.) They also

RIGHT: *The sense of community supported Italian immigrants as they were confronted with the strange realities of life in the New World. This feeling often came through keeping their traditions to eat and share at mealtimes.*

WHEN LIFE IS VERY STRENUOUS AND SPIRITS ARE WAY DOWN
YOU'D BETTER GO TO POLLY'S IN LITTLE GREENWICH TOWN
FOR THERE THE CLANS ARE GATHERED - ITS THERE YOU'LL FIND 'EM ALL
THE ARTISTS AND THE WRITERS RANGED ALONG THE WALL.
MISS POLLY TAKES THE MONEY AND MIKE SAYS HE JUST CAN'T
WAIT ANY FASTER ON THE FOLKS IN POLLY'S RES-TAU-RANT
J.T.B.

GREENWICH VILLAGE _ NEW YORK

JESSIE TARBOX BEA

used peppers, a vegetable unobtainable in Italy in the early twentieth century—as in sausage and peppers, another Italian-American innovation.

Italian immigrants also brought pizza with them to the New World, and this perennial favorite underwent its own transformation. A popular snack food in Naples, Neapolitan pizza is very different from what is eaten in the United States today, having a thinner crust and a lighter topping of just tomato sauce and mozzarella cheese. When Neapolitan bakers set up shops in New York (and other cities), they used leftover dough for pizza, but the first dedicated pizzeria in the New World opened in 1905—Lombardi's at 53 Spring Street in New York City, which offered pizza made by Gennaro Lombardi. New Haven, Connecticut, makes a rival claim as the birthplace of American pizza. Frank Pepe was another New Haven pioneer: His pizza was so popular that he opened a restaurant, Pepe's, on Wooster Street in 1925.

American pizza has evolved in many different ways over the years. More like a large pie, it is no longer a street snack (although a slice "to go" makes a quick bite). The dough base is thicker, and the toppings are more generous and more lavish, with lots of sauce, cheese, and other delights such as pepperoni, anchovies, meatballs, peppers, mushrooms, or whatever takes the chef's (or the patron's) fancy. And in the 1940s, Chicago's Pizzeria Uno invented the deep-dish pizza, which has since spread around the world.

LEFT: *This bakery sells pizza by the slice, just as bakeries did in the old country.*

RIGHT: *Italian fruit ices and ice cream were very popular on the streets of New York.*

LEFT: *Chicago's Pizzeria Uno invented the deep-dish pizza in the 1940s.*

RELIGION

Roman Catholic religious traditions have always been important to Italians, and although it took a while for these practices to be totally accepted in America, their loyalty to the church has not altered since they first arrived in the United States more than 500 years ago. The Catholic Church united Italian immigrant communities, as the common faith and religious observances overcame Old World regional differences. It also helped to cement links across social groups and even generations, providing a common ground for immigrants and their Americanized descendants.

Roman Catholic rituals (from masses to processions) and saints (from St. Rocco to St. Filomena) have inspired the devotion of all Italian Catholics whether they live in Italy or America. The faith of Italians has been strengthened through sacramentals such as crucifixes, rosaries, and scapulars. Pictures of Jesus, Mary, and Joseph, as well as pictures of the many saints and stories of their virtues and sacrifices, have inspired devotion down through the ages. Displays of this devotion have been a recognizable feature of Italian-American life.

Food and religion—two central aspects of Italian-American life—coincide on *festas*, or feast days of saints. The day of the *festa* is filled with acts of piety and devotion. It commences with a vigil on the eve of the feast day, and early the next morning Italians go to church for confession and to attend a special mass for the saint. Those who seek miracles or help through the saint's intercession pray directly to that saint, often standing before his or her shrine where they may light a candle and then kneel or stand to pray before the saint's statuary image.

A *festa* may also include a procession of the saint's image through the streets and end with a shared meal. The feast day of St. Joseph (March 19) includes a display of the most exquisite foods available: a cornucopia of good things to eat such as luscious fruit, cakes, cheeses, olives, cookies, pies, fish, bread, and wine.

Some *festas*, like the festival of San Gennaro, are celebrated in hundreds of towns and cities across the country every year, and they are a source of pleasure not only for the Italian-American community but also for their neighbors. On a large scale, these festivals create a carnival atmosphere, with vendors selling religious articles and plenty of food and drink. At such events, as well as on other occasions, Italian Americans play some of the traditional games of the immigrant generation, such as *bocce*, a game similar to American bowling but played with smaller balls; a card game called *scopa*; and *mora*, the well-known finger game of chance.

RIGHT: *The festa of San Gennaro is celebrated annually in New York City, with processions and a carnival atmosphere.*

RIGHT INSET: *During the San Gennaro festival, churches are ornamented with lights and other decorations.*

LEFT: *After World War II, the G.I Bill was passed, bringing opportunties for education and career development.*

BELOW: *During this time, more Italian immigrants were seen in white-collar occupations than ever before.*

POSTWAR WORK

The end of World War II and the enactment of the G.I. Bill opened up a world of opportunity for many Italian Americans. The war took hundreds of thousands of young men away from their homes and neighborhoods on an unprecedented scale and drafted them into the service of their country as part of a team. This made them think differently about America and how they fitted into the scheme of things. Most were sent to fight in Asia and the Pacific, and others served in Europe and in areas of national security. After the war, President Roosevelt's G.I. Bill came into force, providing returning servicemen and women with financing for a college education or vocational training and for buying a home. The postwar prosperity that fired the economy for many years permitted numerous Italian Americans to open their own family businesses and launch new careers.

By the 1960s national statistics showed that for the first time there were more Italians working in white-collar occupations than in blue-collar jobs. This was a far cry from the days when most Italians could find employment only as menial laborers on the railroads, in factories, in mills, or on farms. By the year 2000, Italian Americans were as well educated and prosperous as other Americans and could be found working in fields as varied as education, the arts, science, technology, commerce, and government service. And although many Italians identify less than some other nationalities with their ethnic traditions, they still have a sense of group cohesion and favor the promotion of Italian culture. This is why large Italian fraternal societies, such as the Sons of Italy, the Italo-American National Union, the Laborers Union, and the Catholic-oriented Knights of Columbus, continue to attract new members.

BELOW: *For many jobs, immigrants needed to speak good English. Here, in this telephone exchange it was imperative.*

Entrepreneurial success

Mention of the world of work would not be complete without a discussion of the high rate of success that Italian Americans have enjoyed in the field of commerce. The California gold rush of 1849 attracted the first wave of Italian immigration to the United States. Known as *L'Altra Italia* (the "other Italy"), thanks to its Mediterranean-like climate, this western state became the most profitable home in the country for Italians. It was in California that northern Italians found an early niche in the fruit and produce business, as well as in farming. One of the first success stories was that of Domenico Ghirardelli (1817–1894), who landed in San Francisco in 1849. He founded his famous factory in 1856 and success in the confec-

tionery trade enabled him and his sons to buy a whole street block, which eventually was named Ghirardelli Square (*see page 65*).

The age-old tradition of wine making was another natural choice for Italian entrepreneurs. Italians were soon able to earn great wealth with the founding of many of the state's leading wineries. In 1881, Andrea Sbarbaro established the Italian-Swiss Colony winery in Sonoma County, and the Napa Valley soon boasted of the Sebastiani and Martini winery. Farther south, in the Central Valley, the Petri and Cribari wineries have flourished alongside the famous Ernest and Julio Gallo winery, which dates from 1933 (*see page 62*).

The rags-to-riches story of Italian immigrant Ettore Boiardi (1897–1985) is an example of the

LEFT: *Here, Angelo Favoretto makes dandelion wine following an old recipe on his Vineland farm* (see page 58).

RIGHT: *Many Italians established successful farms and agricultural businesses across America, such as this cranberry farm in New Jersey.*

"American Dream" coming to life. Born in Borgonovo, a small town in Emilia, Boiardi was a typical Italian immigrant who arrived at Ellis Island in 1914. After passing through immigration, the 16-year-old joined his older brother Ricardo, who was waiting on tables at the impressive Plaza Hotel; Ricardo got Ettore a job as a kitchen boy there. After holding numerous jobs in other fancy hotels, Ettore moved to Cleveland, where he married. In 1929 he and Ricardo opened the Italian Garden Restaurant, which—thanks to Ettore's tomato sauce—became a sensation. In 1936, with help from Ricardo and a third brother, Mario, Ettore founded the Chef Boy-Ar-Dee brand of canned pasta. His products made him a famous millionaire and his picture appeared on every can.

ABOVE: *The food business was a natural focus for Italian immigrants, who imported their favorite products from the old country.*

LEGENDARY ITALIAN AMERICANS

Italian Americans have made outstanding contributions to the history of the United States in all walks of life—science, the arts, culture, and politics. This chapter recalls some of the most famous, but it is by no means exhaustive.

SCIENCE

Without the achievements of three Italian immigrants, America would have not advanced as far as it has in physics and biology. Enrico Fermi (1901–1954) was already an outstanding nuclear physicist—in fact, he had just won the Nobel Prize in his field—when he fled from Mussolini's fascist rule to the United States in December 1938. Following the adoption of Aryan laws in Italy, Fermi feared for the fate of his Jewish wife, and so they sailed to New York to escape any threat. Immediately on arrival he was invited to continue his work at Columbia University, eventually moving to the University of Chicago. His subsequent role in persuading the U.S. government to finance atomic energy research enabled him to construct America's first nuclear reactor in 1942. Later work with a team of distinguished colleagues resulted in completion of the atomic bomb at Los Alamos in 1945.

One of Fermi's pupils also fled from Italy, the brilliant physicist Emilio Segre (1905–1989). Based at the University of California, Segre assisted Fermi and other scientists in the development of the atomic bomb. But he achieved his greatest fame as codiscoverer of the antiproton, and he shared the Nobel Prize for physics in 1959.

A younger Italian scientist, Salvador Luria (1912–1991), was more interested in virology. His fascination with the behavior of DNA in bacteriophages (viruses that infect bacteria) led him and two colleagues to discover that bacteriophages mutate from one generation to another. Their continued pioneering work in this field and its importance to medical science resulted in their winning the Nobel Prize for medicine in 1969, when it was declared that they had "set the solid foundation on which modern molecular biology rests." Luria's textbook, *General Virology* (1967), became a standard in the field.

RIGHT: *Smoking a pipe, the physicist Emilio Segre attends a conference in 1955. He was part of the team that pioneered modern nuclear research.*

FAR RIGHT: *The physicist Enrico Fermi, seen here at work in his lab, fled Italy's fascist government. In America, he broke new ground in atomic energy research.*

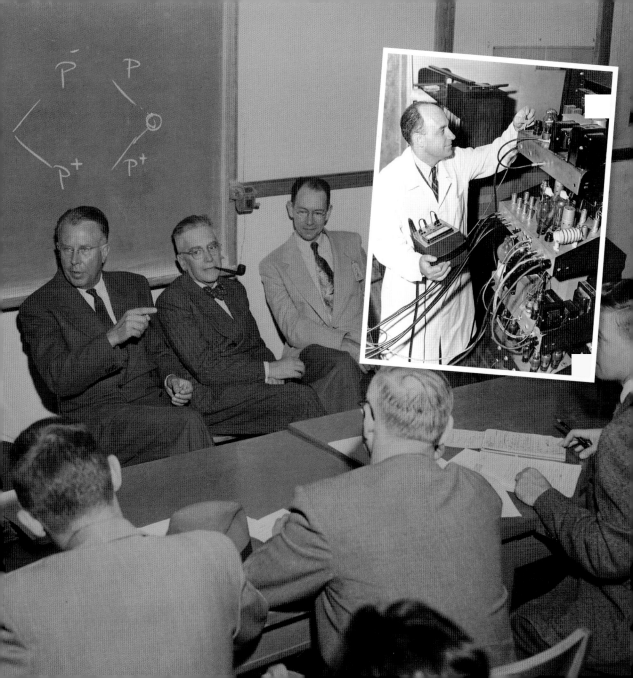

PUBLIC SERVANTS

Although Italian Americans have held high offices in public service since the 1800s, the first to become a legend was indisputably Fiorello H. LaGuardia (1882–1947), New York City's beloved mayor, whose fame was nearly as great as that of President Franklin D. Roosevelt. The son of immigrant parents, he was born Fiorello Raffaele Enrico LaGuardia in Greenwich Village but grew up in Arizona and other western states, where his father was a bandmaster in the U.S. Army. LaGuardia spent his early adult years as a federal employee in the consular service, first in Budapest and then in Fiume, where his position gave him a taste of authority. However, he soon realized that without a proper education he would get nowhere. He returned to New York and enrolled in evening classes at New York University Law School.

Thanks to his knowledge of several foreign languages—Italian, German, Yiddish, French, and Serbo-Croat—LaGuardia was able to get a day job as an immigration interpreter at Ellis Island, although his defense of detained and excluded aliens made life difficult for his superiors. After passing the bar in 1910, he became involved in Republican politics; he was the third Italian American in U.S. history to serve as a member of Congress (1917–1919 and 1923–1933) and the first to serve as mayor of New York (1934–1945). During his mayoral administration he fought corruption, organized crime, and

ABOVE: *Fiorello La Guardia makes one of the many speeches as mayor of New York City. He famously fought corruption and organized crime.*

poverty. Although he charmed the general public and the press with his histrionics and warmth, his determination made him as many enemies as friends. But, unlike most big-city mayors, LaGuardia's national reputation lived after him.

The daughter of an Italian immigrant, Geraldine Ferraro is an important female who should also be mentioned. In 1984 she made history by becoming the first woman chosen to run for vice-president on the ticket of the Democratic presidential candidate Walter Mondale. It turned out that Ferraro and Mondale lost to Ronald Regan and George Bush, but her candidacy did much to advance women's opportunities on the political front.

Other mayors

Distinguished Italian-American mayors in the West and the South have included Angelo Rossi, Joseph Alioto, and George Moscone of San Francisco, and Robert S. Maestri and Victor Schiro of New Orleans. The east coast has seen the rise of prominent figures like Frank Rizzo of Philadelphia and Thomas Menino of Boston, and LaGuardia's successors in New York included Vincent R. Impellitteri (1950–1953) and Rudolph W. Giuliani (1993–2001). Giuliani's leadership of the city after the attacks on the World Trade Center on September 11, 2001, and in the days and weeks that followed, earned him national recognition as well as the gratitude of New Yorkers.

Governors

The first Italian-American governor was John O. Pastore of Rhode Island, who later enjoyed a long and distinguished career as a U.S. senator. Other former governors include Michael Di Salle in Ohio, Albert Rossellini in Washington, Foster Furcolo and John Volpe in Massachusetts, Mario Cuomo in New York, and James Florio in New Jersey. Volpe later served as U.S. Secretary of Transportation, and another Italian American, Edward Corsi, saw federal service as Commissioner of Immigration at Ellis Island (1931–1934). And in 1986 an Italian American finally made it to the U.S. Supreme Court when President Reagan appointed Antonin Scalia an associate justice.

LEFT: *Mayor Rudolph Giuliani congratulates rescue workers in Manhattan, on September 17, 2001.*

ABOVE: *The son of Italian immigrants, Antonin Scalia was appointed associate justice in 1986 by Reagan for his legal brilliance and intellectual abilities.*

THE ARTS

Italian Americans have always excelled in the arts, whether that is in architecture (Vito Battista), painting (Joseph Stella, Luigi Lucioni, Ralph Fasanella, and Frank Stella), sculpture (Costantino Brumidi, *see page 14*), or music (Gian-Carlo Menotti and Harry Warren).

Architecture

The case of one Italian immigrant is particularly moving. Simon Rodia (1879–1965) was a construction worker who picked up enough knowledge of architecture and engineering to enable him to design and build the astonishing Watts Towers in South Central Los Angeles. Born in Ribottoli, Campania in 1879, Rodia came to the United States as a laborer in about 1894. He started out working in the coalfields of Pennsylvania and eventually wound up as a construction worker, mainly around San Francisco. He married in about 1902 and had two children but soon left them. After World War I he settled in Los Angeles and in 1921 purchased land in the Watts district, then populated mostly by Anglos, Italians, Japanese, Mexicans, and Germans. Over the years, Rodia's childhood fasci-

LEFT: Costantino Brumidi (see page 14) arrived in the United States in 1852 and became known as the American Michelangelo for his frescoes in the Capitol dome in Washington D.C.

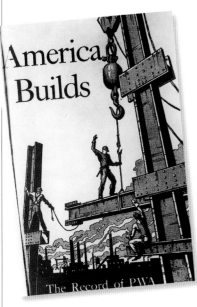

LEFT: *The building boom fostered by the Public Works Administration after the Great Depression created opportunities for Italian American architects and artists.*

RIGHT: *The fantastic Watts Towers, in Los Angeles, California, were designed and built by Simon Rodia, an Italian immigrant.*

nation with great buildings and skyscrapers had created an overpowering desire to build something equally grand with his own hands, and during the next 30 years, working entirely alone, he spent his leisure hours in Los Angeles building what became the tallest structures made by one person. The Watts Towers consist of 17 heavily ornamented sculptures of steel, the tallest of which stands 100 feet high. The ornamentation—all of which is embedded in the metal—consists of broken pottery, tiles, seashells, and glass, After completing his towers in 1954, Rodia moved to northern California where he died in 1965.

Literature

In the early days few immigrants had time to read anything other than newspapers, and the majority could not read at all. Nevertheless, Italian novelists slowly began to appear. Bernardino Cianbelli brought out popular books, such as *I Misteri di Mulberry Street* (*The Mysteries of Mulberry Street*) as early as 1893 and *I Diletti di Bosses* (*Crimes of the Bosses*) in 1895. The period of assimilation saw the rise of novelists like Garibaldi Lapolla (*The Grand Gennaro*, 1932), Pietro di Donato (*Christ in Concrete*, 1939, see page 58), John Fante (*Wait Until Spring, Bandini*, 1938), and John Secondari (*Three Coins in the Fountain*, 1951).

ABOVE: *Author Mario Puzo attends the premiere of* The Godfather, *the acclaimed film based on his novel. The son of Neapolitan immigrants, he was surprised by the success of the book—which sold 21 million copies even before the film was released.*

RIGHT: *The novels of Paul Gallico, the son of an Italian father and an Austrian mother, were always very popular.*

John Fante (1909–1983) went on to achieve greater success when his charming Sicilian-American novel *Full of Life* (1952) was made into a Hollywood movie starring Richard Conte and Judy Holliday. Paul Gallico (1897–1976) won acclaim for his mainstream novels, especially the series featuring an English charwoman, which started with *Mrs. 'Arris Goes to Paris;* then he wrote *The Snow Goose* and *The Poseidon Adventure.* Joseph Tusiani won the Greenwood Prize for his poetry—the first time it had been awarded to an American—and later President John. F. Kennedy invited him to record his poetry (an hour-long tape) for the archives of the Library of Congress in Washington. Contributions to literature were also made by Joe Pagano with *The Golden Wedding*, Mario Puzo with *The Fortunate Pilgrim* and *The Godfather*, Tony Ardizzone with *In the Name of the Father*, and Evan Hunter (Salvatore Lombino) with his Ed McBain detective stories. Prominent nonfiction writers past and present include Gino Speranza, Mario Pei, Gay Talese, Jerre Mangione, Ben Morreale, and Francesco Cordasco.

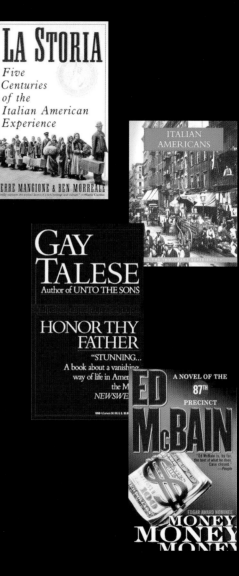

RIGHT: *Italian-American writers have won critical and popular praise for both fiction and nonfiction. Some examples are shown here.*

Music

The world of music attracted a large number of Italian-American singers, composers, and musicians. Arturo Toscanini was an orchestra conductor who set unachievably high standards and was a passionate and dedicated man. Of the American-born singers, the greatest was Mario Lanza (1921–1959), who became a icon for Italian Americans during his sensational career in opera, on the concert stage, in radio, on television, and as a Hollywood star. He was the first singer in recording history to sell 2.5 million records. In one film, *The Great Caruso*, he portrayed his idol, the incomparable Enrico Caruso. His other films include *Because You're Mine*, *That Midnight Kiss*, and *Toast of New Orleans*.

Other popular singing stars included operatic soprano Rosa Ponselle, 1920s pop singer Nick Lucas ("Tip Toe Through the Tulips" and "Bye, Bye Blackbird"), crooner Russ Columbo ("Prisoner of Love"), Ezio Pinza, Perry Como, Frank Sinatra, Dean Martin, Frankie Laine, Tony Bennett, Vic Damone, Bobby Darrin, Fabian, Frankie Avalon, and Frank Zappa. Then there was bandleader Guy Lombardo, pianist Liberace, and composer Henry Mancini. Present Italian-American stars include Bruce Springsteen and Madonna Ciccone, known simply as Madonna.

Most people do not know that one of the most successful songwriters of the Golden Age of Hollywood was an Italian American. This is

ABOVE: *Born in South Philadelphia, Mario Lanza became world famous after starring in many Hollywood films and singing with top opera singers.*

BELOW: *Perry Como started his singing career with the big bands of the 1930s. His 50-year association with the RCA Victor record label began in 1943.*

RIGHT: *Italian-American singing stars Frank Sinatra [left] and Dean Martin [center] with fellow Rat Pack member Peter Lawford.*

because when he was a little boy, his older sisters changed his name from Salvatore Guaragna to Harry Warren (1893–1981). Born in Brooklyn to parents who had emigrated from Calabria in search of a better life, he was typical of the first generation of Italian Americans in feeling anxious to be American but unable to escape his Italianness: "I remember as a child I had no interest in being Italian, only in being American. Strangely, many years later, as an adult, I got to appreciate my Italian background and thought sometimes about going to Italy to live."

Warren wrote more than 300 songs, 50 of which are considered American standards. They include the 1930s hits "Forty Second Street,"

"You're Getting to be a Habit with Me," "I Only Have Eyes for You," "Lullaby of Broadway," "We're in the Money," "September in the Rain," "Jeepers Creepers," and "You Must Have Been a Beautiful Baby." His 1940s' hits include "Chattanooga Choo Choo," "I Had the Craziest Dream," "I Got a Gal in Kalamazoo," "Serenade in Blue," "There Will Never Be Another You," and "You'll Never Know." In the 1950s, before retiring, he wrote "That's Amore" and "Inamorata" for Dean Martin and the theme songs of the classic films *An Affair to Remember* (1957) and *Separate Tables* (1958). In all, Harry Warren produced more American standards than Irving Berlin.

BELOW: *Known to many as "The Boss," Bruce Springsteen's fame rocketed in 1984 with his release of the album "Born in the U.S.A."*

RIGHT: *Born Salvatore Guaragna, Harry Warren's name was changed before he achieved great acclaim as a songwriter from the 1930s to the 1950s.*

ABOVE: *Madonna's brash talent made her one of the most successful recording artists of all time.*

Theater

The vaudeville stage attracted much Italian-American talent, including two legendary comedians, Jimmy Savo and Jimmy Durante. For years, Jimmy Savo (1896–1960), the son of an Italian cobbler, was one of the highest paid performers in vaudeville, thanks to his ability to put on the silliest clothes and sing the funniest songs. He was so short that on stage he looked as if he were standing in a hole. He made his act even funnier by wearing clothes far too big for him, including an enormous derby hat, and carrying an oversized umbrella. He would then gaze at the audience with a sad, wistful smile. He always appeared at a loss in a world that was big and cold, but he could also adopt an impish, sly air that had spectators laughing in the aisles. He could put over a song like no one else could, and audiences clamored to hear him sing "One Meatball," "River, Stay Away From My Door," or "That Old Black Magic." His singing always included plenty of pantomiming, which made his performance amazingly effective. His Broadway shows included *Listen Lester, Vogues of 1924*, and *Mum's the Word.*

The beloved, excitable, irascible king of comedy Jimmy Durante (1893–1980) was originally a piano player but later won fame as a speakeasy comedian in the late 1920s. This led to stardom in films like *Roadhouse Nights*, *What, No Beer?*, and *Jumbo*, and finally in various radio and television shows, such as *Hollywood Palace*. Like Savo

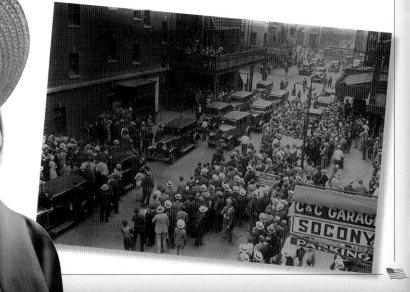

RIGHT: *Alfred Drake, third from left, starred as Curly in the original cast of Oklahoma on Broadway.*

FAR LEFT: *Jimmy Durante was one of the most popular vaudeville acts, and he managed the transition to television without losing a laugh.*

LEFT: *A vast crowd gathers at the stage door of the New Amsterdam Theater, awaiting the arrival of comedian Jimmy Savo, in July 1930.*

and other old-time comedians, Durante became famous for poking fun at his big nose, his famous *schnozzola*. He made a career out of joking about his troubles and was known for his endless routines and for catch phrases such as "I'm mortified," "Did ja ever have da feeling dat ya wanted to go, an' still had da feeling dat ya wanted ta stay?" His manner-

isms and jokes were imitated everywhere, making him a legend in his own lifetime.

Born Alfred Capurro, Broadway star Alfred Drake (1914–1992) preferred dramatic Shakespearean parts, but audiences adored him when he starred in musicals like *Oklahoma!*, *Kiss Me Kate*, and *Kismet*. He also performed in motion pictures.

Motion pictures

Hollywood did not have to wait long for [...]
to make a[...]
silent film [...]
immigrant [...]
(1895–192 [...]
SS Cleveland [...]
in New Yor [...]
newcomers, [...]
year, workir [...]
an Italian gr [...]
in Central P [...]
able to spea [...]
a dancer anc [...]
Glass persua [...]
with her, anc [...]
all the way [...]
down to Los [...]
the team split [...]

Valentino [...]
in 16 films bef [...]
his star potent [...]
Horsemen of the A [...]
at the box offic [...]
was born. Film [...]
"king of Holly...ood" and the "world's greatest

lover." His films included *Camille, The Conquering* [...] *he Sheik, Blood and Sand, Monsieur Beaucaire,* [...] *a;* his final screen role was in *Son of the Sheik.* [...] s (especially *The Sheik*) are said to have [...] onized American culture by making [...] between ethnic groups alluring. One critic [...] t Valentino made "olive skin, oiled hair [...] urns" a major industry and observed that [...] n calling attractive young men "sheiks." [...] spawned many imitators, such as Ramon [...] Ricardo Cortez, and Gilbert Roland. His [...] 26 of peritonitis caused a sensation such [...] previously been seen in New York and [...] s. Valentino left behind a score of imita- [...] egend that has never died.

e advent of sound in motion pictures [...] of new stars, one of the first of whom [...] LaRue (1902–1984). Born Gaspare [...] n New York, LaRue became famous for [...] nacing characters in roles that he [...] the screen in the 1930s and 1940s. [...] performance was perhaps in the social [...] *ry of Temple Drake,* an acknowledged [...] also starred in *A Farewell to Arms,* [...] ...o *Orchids for Miss Blandish,* and *Robin and the Seven Hoods.*

Wisconsin-born Don Ameche (1908–1993) was perhaps the first Italian American to become a major star in the 1930s and 1940s, with many comebacks in later years. His best films include *The Story of Alexander Graham Bell, Gateway,* and *Cocoon.*

LEFT: *Rudolph Valentino defined the concept of the "Latin Lover." His enigmatic performance style won him critical acclaim.*

INSET: *The funeral procession for Rudolph Valentino in 1926. Mystery surrounded his unexpected death at only 31 years old.*

ABOVE: Anchors Aweigh
(1945) was a Hollywood star
vehicle for Frank Sinatra.

He was also a major radio star in the days when radio was still big, performing in *The First Nighter*, *Jack Armstrong*, and *The Bickersons*. On Broadway he starred in Cole Porter's *Silk Stockings* (1955).

In postwar Hollywood Frank Sinatra (1915–1998), who had been a major pop singer since the 1930s, gave outstanding performances in *Anchors Aweigh*, *From Here to Eternity*, *The Manchurian Candidate*, *Robin and the Seven Hoods*, *Oceans Eleven*, and *The Detective*.

With the exception of the Sicilian comedy *Full of Life*, actor Richard Conte (1914–1975) achieved fame chiefly as a leading dramatic actor in films such as *Guadalcanal Diary*, *The Purple Heart*, *Call Northside 777*, and *I'll Cry Tomorrow*.

One of comedy's greatest stars was Lou Costello (1908–1959), whose squeamish comedy technique amused a generation of moviegoers. The characterizations he perfected in burlesque with his stage partner Bud Abbott created classic humor that remains as funny as ever. Abbott and Costello's "Who's on first?" baseball routine gained them national fame when they performed it on radio in 1938. This soon led to film roles that catapulted them to nationwide stardom. Among

LEFT: *The comedy duo of Bud
Abbott [right] and Lou Costello
[left] shone on radio, film,
and television.*

their most hilarious films are *One Night in the Tropics*, *Buck Privates*, *Hold That Ghost*, *The Wistful Widow of Wagon Gap*, and *Abbott and Costello Meet Frankenstein*.

Italian Americans also achieved signal fame as filmmakers. Ellis Island immigrant Frank Capra (1897–1991) directed some of Hollywood's greatest film classics: *It Happened One Night*, *Mr. Deeds Goes to Town*, *You Can't Take It With You*, and *Mr. Smith Goes to Washington*. Other directors following in his footsteps include Francis Ford Coppola and Martin Scorsese. And in the field of cartoons, entertainment would never have been the same without Woody Woodpecker, the creation of Walter Lantz (originally Lanza), another son of Italian immigrants.

RIGHT: *Italian immigrant Frank Capra directed such cinema classics as* Mr. Deeds Goes to Town, *which presents an idealized view of American life.*

BELOW: *A intricate tale of family relationship and organized crime,* The Godfather *was based on the novel by Italian American author Mario Puzo (see page 104).*

BELOW: *The Oscar-winning, acclaimed director, Francis Ford Coppola.*

SPORT

As in show business, Italian Americans also scored highly in sports. The legendary Charles Atlas (1893–1972) was the father of body-building. He was born Angelo Siciliano in Acri, a town in southern Italy, and emigrated through Ellis Island with his mother. Growing up in Brooklyn, he developed his "dynamic tension" exercises, which gave him the strength he craved and enabled him to work as a strongman at Coney Island, as an artist's model in Greenwich Village, and eventually as a gym trainer. With a business adviser, he developed his now-famous mail-order exercise program. The company's most famous advertisement was one in which a strong bully kicks sand into the face of a skinny boy, humiliating him in front of his girlfriend; but soon after completing the Charles Atlas muscle-developing program, the boy returns and gets his revenge—and plenty of girlfriends as well. The advertisements attracted male readers with questions like "Do you want to be a tiger?" and Atlas made a fortune as the promoter of isometric exercises.

Other Italians who achieved fame in sports include baseball legends Joe DiMaggio, Dominic DiMaggio, Yogi Berra, Joe Garagiola, and Tommy LaSorda; champion boxers Rocky Marciano, Rocky Graziano, and Jake La Motta; world-famous jockey Eddie Arcaro; champion golfer Gene Sarazen; and football stars Joe Montana and Dan Marino.

BELOW: *Marketing his exercise program in the media, Charles Atlas, an Italian immigrant, became famous across the nation for his phenomenal physique. He was known as the "world's most perfectly developed male."*

RIGHT: *Joe DiMaggio, the son of a Genoese immigrant who settled in San Francisco, was one of the biggest stars of baseball and an American icon.*

FAR RIGHT: *Other Italian-American sports heroes include, the boxer Rocky Marciano, the boxer Jake LaMotta (seen here as portrayed by Robert De Niro in Raging Bull), and Joe Montana, quarterback for the San Francisco 49ers.*

RELIGION

Although Italian-American priests have faced a stone wall in their hope of attaining advancement in the Catholic hierarchy in the United States, they have nonetheless made important contributions to the faith through works of charity, piety, and service. Leading Italian-American priests have included Cardinal Archbishops Joseph L. Bernardin of Chicago and Anthony Bevilacqua of Philadelphia, and Archbishop Silvanio Tomasi, a Scalabrinian scholar.

St. Frances Cabrini: Patroness of immigrants

One of the holiest American Catholics was Francesca Xavier Cabrini, who was canonized in 1946 and is the saint to whom all immigrants may have recourse. Maria Francesca Cabrini was born in Lombardy on July 15, 1850. In 1880 she founded the Missionary Sisters of the Sacred Heart. As its Mother Superior, she established a convent and by 1887 had set up several orphanages and schools to aid poor Italian children. That year she was received by Pope Leo XIII, who was deeply impressed by her work and pleased to learn of her interest in missionary work abroad. For some time, the exodus of thousands of *contadini* had been troubling his mind, and he saw in Mother Cabrini the perfect instrument of the church in bringing succor to them.

Blessed by the Holy Father, she sailed to New York with six of her nuns, where she found Italians living in slums with little help. Although Italian Franciscan priests ministered at the parishes of St. Anthony of Padua and Our Lady of Pompeii, most

LEFT: *Mother Frances Xavier Cabrini became the first American saint, canonized in 1946, for her efforts in founding schools and orphanages.*

ABOVE: *Mother Cabrini's body lies in state in 1947 in the chapel of the high school in New York City that bears her name.*

LEFT: *Four-year-old Edward Unish prays before the shrine of Mother Cabrini—his mother believed that the prayers she had said before the shrine brought about the cure of her young son, who had been born paralyzed.*

of the *contadini* depended on Irish priests. Mother Cabrini was appalled by the wretchedness she found in Little Italy: abandoned children roaming the streets in rags, eating from garbage cans, and begging in shop doorways. With help from Italian shopkeepers, she was able to provide care for many of them and later established an orphanage. She made trips to Italy, bringing over more nuns in 1890 and 1891.

By 1892 she had raised enough money to open Columbus Hospital (called Cabrini Medical Center since 1958) for Italian immigrants. Seven years later, she opened what is now known as Cabrini High School. Then she began to expand her activities in Little Italies throughout the country, founding a convent and orphanage in New Orleans; a Catholic school in Boston; missions and hospitals in Chicago, Newark, and Arlington; and Catholic schools in Brooklyn, Hartford, Scranton, Denver, Seattle, and Los Angeles. She also founded missions and hospitals in Wyoming, Nicaragua, and Brazil. She became a naturalized U.S. citizen in 1909 and died in Chicago in December 1917 while wrapping Christmas gifts. She was beatified in 1938 and raised to sainthood by Pope Pius XII in 1949; her feast day is November 13.

HERITAGE

A QUESTION OF IDENTITY

By choosing the United States as their permanent home and not just as a source of temporary work, Italians chose well, for they found themselves in a land where the potential for liberty and wealth was far greater than in just about any other country in the world. Even the fear of losing their connection with the old life in Italy was not enough to sway those who took the plunge. Although they encountered unfriendliness, prejudice, and resistance from all too many Americans, Italians quietly persisted in creating new homes for their families. Sustained by their resilience and optimism, they found the means to make life worth living.

Their American-born children were confronted by new challenges. One was the question of identity: Who were they, and what did they want to be—Italians or Americans? The choice proved far more problematic than it might appear on the surface, for these youngsters' parents remained extremely Italian and always had a tremendous sense of their own nationality. But the young people were torn between loyalty to the old ways and the swift, aggressive assimilation into mainstream society that was so much a part of the world around them. They were called on to make

profoundly important personal decisions—decisions with which they struggled: Where to live, what line of work to take up, whether or not to attend college, and whom to marry.

The decision whether to marry within or outside the Italian community was often vital to their lives. Studies show that an unusually large number of Italians chose to marry outside their ethnicity. For many, this was an important way to break into American society, which might otherwise have remained closed to them. From these matches came children who were not usually brought up with Italian values and customs as their sole point of reference; this was their parents' great sacrifice to Americanization. For those who chose to marry another Italian American, keeping the family traditions going was easier; their only problem was that their own children often did not acquire a wider education or a broader cultural experience. Both groups were subject to the strain of living between two worlds. At times traditional Italians might suffer from the fear that America could never quite be their homeland, whereas those who moved further into mainstream society might occasionally feel a pang of loss or a lack of rootedness, and a sense of being neither Italian nor American enough. But as younger generations came

BELOW: *Many Italian Americans visit Italy for vacations, to reconnect with their roots in the Old Country, as here in Pompeii.*

ABOVE: *These girls, at the festival of St. Anthony in Wilmington, Delaware, are maintaining a long tradition of celebrating festas* (see page 92).

along, this source of stress began to vanish and gradually was forgotten.

For today's Italian Americans, the decision has been made and they have become Americans first and foremost. For some a sense of loss persists, whereas for others only curiosity draws them to confront their Italian heritage. The way of recapturing their Italianness takes many forms. Some have taken up Italian in college; others travel with tour groups to Italy or study Italian history and culture. Another means of satisfying this yearning to reconnect with a world that has been lost has emerged over the past 25 years or so and attracts more and more Americans of Italian ancestry each year: the study of genealogy.

Genealogy has encouraged scores of people to study their family history. Family history enthusiasts can now track down the movement of great-grandparents and grandparents long gone; for the lucky ones, some of these old timers are still around today and can relate bits and pieces of forgotten history and lore. Younger generations can look back in respect at the struggles and sacrifices their families made, both in America and in Italy, or in Italian communities in Switzerland, France, or South America. Through factual evidence discovered in family documents—old passports, the booklet of a journeyman apprentice, character testimonials, steamship receipts, betrothal contracts, and marriage certificates—the veil of the past is slowly being drawn aside, and the stories and accomplishments of these legendary people are coming alive.

Over the past 50 years, Italian Americans have moved into jobs and professions of every kind. Where previously they were mostly unskilled laborers and sometimes artisans, they can now be found as a major presence in many fields. Today they are counted among the most successful stockbrokers, executives, professionals, and artists in America. Their success demonstrates that they can only continue to advance and their strength and self-confidence have increased with the growing appreciation of their cultural heritage by people from all walks of life.

Italian culinary traditions have been given a sense of place and recommendation in America—a remarkable development considering that Italian food was previously restricted to Little Italies and other neighborhoods with an Italian population. Not so today. Starting in the 1950s, pizza parlors have spread quickly throughout the nation as Italian entrepreneurs recognized the demand and opened restaurants wherever there were customers. Packaged Italian food had already introduced scores of non-Italians to Italian food styles, and finding the materials to make a home-cooked Italian meal is now as easy as going to any market in America, where there will be a variety of pasta, cheeses, fresh herbs, and tomato sauce preparations in abundant display.

Today's Italian Americans have kept much of their ancestral Italian zest, although now a blend of other influences they have a bright new lustre. They have both an Italian and an American heritage, for which they can be duly proud in equal measure. They have preserved many of the finest traditions and most cherished customs and beliefs brought to America by their great-grandparents, from loyalty to the teachings of the Roman Catholic Church to the love of good Italian food and wine. Their contributions as Americans are myriad: They have been laborers and pioneers in a variety of fields; they have been skilled craftspeople and artists; they have built factories and businesses; they have been intellectuals and teachers. Yet in their search for acceptance they endured many injustices: mockery, discrimination, and continuous stereotyping, to name but a few. However, they have proved their unstinting loyalty and patriotism—often beyond the call of duty. With such a past, Italian Americans can embrace new challenges as America moves ahead in the twenty-first century. And they can look back with gratitude on a rich heritage.

RIGHT: *Although Italian Americans celebrate their cultural heritage, they are loyal to the United States. Here, members of the Supreme Council of the Order of the Sons of Italy salute the Liberty Bell in 1941.*

TIMELINE

1492 Italian-born Spanish explorer Cristoforo Colombo arrives in America and claims it for Spain.

1505 The Italian-born Spanish explorer Amerigo Vespucci visits America; the New World later named in his honor.

1848 Italian immigrants are attracted to the United States after gold is discovered in California.

1849 *L'Eco d'Italia*, America's first Italian language newspaper, begins weekly publication in New York.

LEFT: *Immigrants shown having just disembarked from their ship.*

1855 The Castle Garden immigration station opens in New York.

1862 The Homestead Act encourages immigration by granting 160 acres of land to successful applicants.

1880 In New York City, Carlo Barsotti establishes the first Italian daily newspaper—*Il Progresso Italo-Americano*. It became the most influential Italian paper in the country.

1889 Mother Francesca Xavier Cabrini goes to America to begin her lifelong work of helping Catholic immigrants.

1890 Castle Garden through which an estimated 300,000 Italians had been processed, closes.

1891 Pope Leo XIII opens a New York branch of the San Raffaele Society

1892 Ellis Island immigration station opens in New York harbor.

1901 In New York, prominent Italian Americans, led by attorney Gino Speranza, found the Society for the Protection of Italian Immigrants, to protect Italian immigrants from potential exploitation.

1917 A new U.S. Immigration law is enacted requiring those entering the country to be literate in their own language. The U.S. enters World War I on the allied side led by France, the U.K. and Italy.

1922 Italian King Vittorio Emmanuelle III appoints Benito Mussolini prime minister.

RIGHT: *Frank Capra directed many Hollywood film classics including,* You Can't Take it With You *(see page 113).*

1924 The U.S. enacts an immigration law to severely curtail immigration numbers to only 153,774 people per year. The Italian quota was set at 3, 845 annually.

1927 Controversial execution of Italian immigrants Sacco and Vanzetti for murder in Massachusetts.

1933 Fiorello La Guardia is elected mayor of New York City, serving until 1946.

1939 Publication of Pietro di Donato's best-selling novel, *Christ in Concrete,* the story of the struggles of an Italian immigrant family.

1941 Italy declares war against the United States. President Roosevelt signs an executive order designating "enemy aliens" as all Italian citizens residing in America. This effected 600,000 people; but only a few thousand were interrogated or detained at Ellis Island and other federal detention facilities.

1942–1945 An estimated 500,000 Italian Americans serve in the armed forces during World War II, many of whom are decorated with the Congressional Medal of Honor and the Navy Cross.

1943 King Vittorio Emmanuelle deposes Mussolini and ends Italy's alliance with Nazi Germany.

1946 The notorious gangster Charles "Lucky" Luciano is released from Ellis Island and deported to Italy.

1950 Rhode Island governor John O. Pastore becomes the first Italian American to be elected a United States Senator.

1954 Ellis Island closes.

1970–1974 240,000 Americans of Italian descent are reported in the federal census, more than half of whom reside in the northeastern states.

1984 Congresswoman Geraldine Ferraro is nominated as the Democratic candidate for vice president of the United States, but is defeated in the general election.

RESOURCES

FURTHER READING

Di Franco, J. Philip. *The Italian Americans*. New York: Chelsea House Publishers, 1988.

Foerster, Robert F. *The Italian Emigration of Our Times*. Cambridge:Harvard University Press, 1919.

Hoobler, Dorothy and Thomas. *The Italian-American Family Album*. New York: Oxford University Press, 1994.

Italian-American Tribune (newspaper). Newark, New Jersey. www.italiantribune.com

LaGumina, Salvatore (ed.). *Wop!: A Documentary History of Anti-Italian Discrimination*. Toronto: Guernica Editions, 1999.

————. *The Immigrants Speak: Italian Americans Tell Their Story*. Staten Island, New York: Center for Migration Studies, 1979.

La Sorte, Michael. *La Merica: Images of Italian Greenhorn Experience*. Philadelphia: Temple University Press, 1985.

Lord, Eliot, et al. *The Italian in America*. New York: B.F. Buck and Company, 1905.

Mangione, Jerre, and Morreale, Ben. *La Storia*. New York: Harper Collins, 1992.

Nelli, Humbert. 'Italians' in *Harvard Encyclopedia of American Ethnic Groups*. (editors Stephen Thernstrom and Ann Orlov). Cambridge: Harvard University Press, 1980.

Pitkin, Thomas M. *Keepers of the Gate: A History of Ellis Island*. New York: New York University Press, 1975.

Rosoli, Gianfausto. *L'Altra Italia: Storia Fotografica della Grande Emigrazione Italiana nelle Americhe, 1880–1915*. Rome: Centro Studi Emigrazione, 1970.

Schoener, Allon. *The Italian Americans*. New York: Macmillan Publishing Company, 1987.

ASSOCIATIONS AND ORGANIZATIONS

American-Italian Heritage Association
P.O. Box 3136
Albany, NY 12203-0136
www.aiha-albany.org

Embassy of Italy in the United States
3000 Whitehaven Street, N.W.
Washington, DC 20008
www.italyemb.org

John D. Calandra Italian-American Institute
25 West 43rd Street, 18th Floor
New York, NY 10036
www.qc.edu/calandra

Museo Italo Americano
Fort Mason Center, Building C
San Francisco, CA 94123
www.museoitaloamericano.org

Order of the Sons of Italy
219 E Street, N.E.
Washington, D.C. 20002
www.osia.org

WEB SITES

Italian-Americans.com (www.italianamericans.com)
Provides language lessons, club names and addresses, photographs of Italy, events, and more.

Italian-Americans: The Immigrant Experience (www.hlla.com/catalog/italamer.html)
Provides excerpts from The Immigrant Experience Series on Internet sites in genealogy, history, culture, social commentary, associations, language, travel, and maps, and more.

Italian-American Web Site of New York (www.italian-american.com/main.htm)
A multimedia site with numerous links to organizations, genealogy, history, politics, feasts, famous Italians, and more.

Italian American Heritage Foundation (www.iahfsj.org)
This society introduces its activities, events, festivals with links to online Italian newspapers, radio and tv, music, opera and theater, embassies, and more.

National Italian American Foundation (www.niaf.org)
Main advocate in Washington, D.C. for Italian Americans, provides information on programs, conventions, research, reports, and more.

Italian-American Clubs and Organizations (www.italianclubs.com)
Handy directory of links to Italian history, culture, festivals, and businesses.

Acknowledgments

This book is dedicated to the memory of King Vittorio Emmanuelle II. I wish to express my gratitude to Eric Byron, Jeffrey Dosik, and Janet Levine who work with me at Ellis Island. I also appreciate the encouragement of General Mario Arpino, retired commander of the Italian Air Force; and finally a thank you to Giovanna and Francesca Soro, two natives of Sardinia who, during their visit from Italy, very kindly shared their family emigration stories.

PHOTO CREDITS
Archiv fur Kunst und Geschicte, London: pp. 43, 66, 83, 88, 89 both, 91M.
Cameron Collections: pp. 8B, 9, 10, 12, 16, 54, 62B, 64B.
Corbis: pp. 11T Archivo Iconografico, SA,19B, 22 Michael Maslan Historical Photographs, 23 Archivo Iconografico,SA, 24 Histoircal Picture Archive, 26T Hulton-Deutsch, 29B The Mariners Museum, 32, 32/3 Underwood &Underwood, 41T Michael Maslan Historical Photos, 48, 49, 50/1, 56 April Saul, 57L Robert Holmes, 57R Ed Eckstein, 58 Michael S Yamashita, 59 Todd Gipstein, 60 Robert Holmes, 61, 63B Lake County Museum, 64T, 65 Morton Beebe, 69 Bowers Museum of Cultural Art, 73, 74 Underwood & Underwood, 79T, 81 Underwood & Underwood, 84 Hulton-Deutsch, 91B Kelly-Mooney Photography, 93 inset Farell Grehan, 93 and 96, Bob Krist, 97 Catherine Karnow, 99, 100, 101L Mike Stewart/Sygma, 102 Wally McNamee, 107 John Springer, 108L Jerry Cooke, 112B Cinema Photo, 119L Roger Ressmeyer, 119R Kevin Fleming.
Corbis/Bettmann: pp. 7, 18, 21, 26, 28, 29T, 30, 34, 36, 31B, 44B, 46, 47, 53L, 53R, 63, 68, 73R, 75, 76T, 77 both, 80, 82 both, 83 inset, 84/5, 85R, 99, 101R, 193, 104 both, 108R, 109, 110B, 114, 115B, 116, 117 both,120.

INDEX